Expression and Literature: Common Tumbuka Ideophones and their Usage

Copyright 2015 Songiso Mvalo

All rights reserved. No part of this publication may be reproduced, stored in a retrieval system, or transmitted in any form or by any means, electronic, mechanical, photocopying, recording or otherwise, without prior permission from the publishers.

Published by

Mzuni Press
P/Bag 201
Luwinga, Mzuzu 2

ISBN 978-99908-0243-6

Mzuni Press is represented outside Africa by:

African Books Collective Oxford (orders@africanbookscollective.com)

www.mzunipress.luviri.com
www.mzunipress.blogspot.com
www.africanbookscollective.com

Printed in Malawi by Baptist Publications, P.O. Box 444, Lilongwe

Expression and Literature: Common Tumbuka Ideophones and their Usage

William Edward Songiso Mvalo

MZUNI PRESS

Mzuni Books no. 19

Mzuzu

2015

PREFACE

Tumbuka is the dominant language in the Northern Region of Malawi. It is, however, also spoken in large pockets of Kasungu District in the Central Region and also in the Eastern Province of Zambia, and in Lundazi District in particular. Tonga, spoken in Nkhatabay and Nkhotakota, is like a cousin to Tumbuka with a close resemblance in their phonetics.

Although Tumbuka is spoken that widely in the North, there are a lot more languages in Karonga and Chitipa apart from Tumbuka. In Karonga there are Nyakyusa and Nkhonde, in Chitipa we find Namwanga, Lambya, Sukwa, Nyiha and Ndali, amongst others.

Rumphi District, however, can boast of unadulterated Tumbuka, though a small pocket speaks Phoka which, however, is clearly understood by any Tumbuka speaker. A large portion of Mzimba District has a mixture of Tumbuka, Nguni, and Tonga resulting, at times, in formulation of words said in one area with a different intonation, but meaning the same thing, e.g. **nikhumba and ndikhumba** in Mzimba South and Nkhata Bay (where there is a lot of language interface with Tonga) and **nkhukhumba** in Mzimba North and Rumphi, or **nihamba** (in Mzimba South) and **nkhuhamba** (in Mzimba North) where there is also a lot of Tumbuka and Nguni interface – adopted from the Nguni verb **kuhamba – to go**. In some instances, there are formulations of words that are peculiar to some limited area within the district (e.g. **uyankhu** in Mzimba South as opposed to **ukuyankhu** in Rumphi), but meaning the same: "where are you going?" The result is that some Tumbuka words used in one part of Mzimba may seem strange to words used in Rumphi.

Like other Bantu languages, Tumbuka is also very expressive, but can also be very economic in communication or use of words, and yet clearly delivering the desired message. This can be done through the use of idioms, proverbs, or ideophones. **This collection is on commonly used Tumbuka ideophones, where an ideophone shall mean "a word describing a situation, or a state of affairs, or a set of actions – all in one word."** These words are derived mostly from verbs and sometimes from nouns – **e.g. lingu/lingizge** (from the verbs –**kulingizga or kulingula** – to peep), or **lwaha** – the act of inattentiveness (from the noun **chilwaha**). Some ideophones, however, stand on their own – **e.g. beng'ende** (being nude). Other ideophones can be repeated **e.g. bilinkhinyu.**[2] Said once, it denotes a single act of wriggling. If repeated – **bilinkhinyu-bilinkhinyu (or bilinkhinyu**[2]**)** – it is in reference to continued motions of wriggling as in the movement of a worm.

The letters "l" and "r" are easily interchangeable in Tumbuka – **e.g. "lopolopo"** and **"roporopo," "lakalaka"** and **"rakaraka."** Both mean the same thing – dropping in abundance.

Because some ideophones do not have a direct English translation, it is hoped that where these occur, the explanations given will closely relate to some English meaning, for instance, in the ideophone **"pyepyetu"** from the verb **"kupyepyetula,"** to knock down someone from their feet.

Notes:

(1) A superscript ^{2} or ^{3} indicates that the ideophone has a single expression and a double or triple one.

(2) Pronunciation: The Tumbuka language distinguishes between a soft and a hard b. In this book the soft b is expressed as ŵ, and in the alphabetical sequence of the ideophones it follows directly after the hard b.

ACKNOWLEDGEMENTS

I am indebted to Late Tito Banda, then from the Department of Languages and Literature who, after reviewing the very first raw manuscript, encouraged me to forge ahead as what I had started would be a rich and unique contribution to Tumbuka Literature. Professor Boston Soko and Associate Professor Fred Nkhwendavibe Msiska both examined the final manuscript and they too encouraged me to ensure that the collection is published as it was both inspiring and stimulating and that the methodology was good. Colleagues at the Mzuzu Golf Club, thank you all as, without your knowledge, I was collecting these ideophones as we laughed and joked over social and political issues. I also wish to thank Ms. Linda Golosi for her meticulous efforts in the setting and typing the manuscript. Lastly, I am particularly indebted to Professor Klaus Fiedler who formatted the book with a professional editorial comb to ensure that both presentation and readability flow.

Ba or Bamu

These are derived from the verb 'kubamuka' to suddenly get through a barrier to clearance – as in going through a forest and suddenly onto a clearance or road.

'ba' or *'bamu'* is in reference to breaking through.

"Uko tikuchimbira nkhalamo muthengele, mbwenu mwamwawi mumusewu ba/bamu."

Babaku

This comes from the verbs "kubabakula" or "kubabakuka" to pull in one's stomach.

"*babaku*" is in reference to that retraction of one's stomach, or as with a cobra, its neck when it is ready to spit.

"Uyu mwana njala yakoma – awonani kumutima kuli babaku."

"Awonani vuvi wachita kuti singo babaku!"

Bafu

This comes from the verb "kubafula" to kick with the foot.

"*bafu*" refers to that act of kicking or striking something with the foot.

"Apo Lazalo wakati wayezge kukaka ng'ombe na goda, mbwenu yili naye bafu."

Bagada-bagada

"*bagada-bagada*" is in reference to the unsteady or unstable walk either in a person or as with a duck.

"Chifukwa cha matekenya, Chiukepo pakwenda sono ni bagada-bagada."

Bagadale

This is from the verb "kubagadala" to be out of form, or not in a straight neat row or line because of being in excess – as in teeth *(also see "pangalale")*.

"*bagadale*" is in reference to teeth or stakes or feet not being straight or not being in a neat row because they are too many.

"Achiwoneni ŵati, mumulomo mino bagadale ngati ŵali kuchita kufwindamo!"

"Tamala watowelechi, kweni mbwenu malundi bagadale!"

Balala[2]/balari[2]

This stems from the verb "kubalaliska" to scatter or to throw about in various directions (also see "chunkhu").

"*balala*" or "*balari*" is in reference to a scenario where things are "all over" or "scattered all over" or "being in a disorderly form" or – in slang – "incoherent" as in thoughts or argument.

"Ng'ombe zati zachiluka, mbwenu balala/balari."

"Ŵati ŵamutangwaniska na mafumbo Yezgani, mbwenu fundo zose balala."

Banankhu

This comes from the verb "kubanankhula" to open forcibly or to dismantle.

"*banankhu*" is in reference to the snap or the sudden release of a latch or a lock on a door.

"Soyaphi wakalimbana nacho chijalo mpaka kabali banankhu."

Bang'anthu

This is from the verb "kubang'anthula" also to open forcibly *(see "banankhu")*.

'*bang'anthu*' as also in '*banankhu*' refers to the sudden snap of a latch or lock or door.

"Wanangwa wakatimba chijalo na musi mpaka chijalo bang'anthu."

Banthu

This comes from the verb "kubanthula" to detach or to break off a piece.

'*banthu*' is in reference to the detachment or the separation of a piece from the main.

"Apo wakaseŵeleskanga kang'ombe kake kakuwumba, mbwenu kalipondo banthu."

Banu

This word comes from the verb "kubanula" to open (could be eyes, legs etc) or the verb "kubanuka" to realize or to become aware.

'*banu*' refers to the opening of eye lids, or the sudden realization of a truth or a solution. It can also be used in reference to the opening up of thighs.

"Muhanya uno ndipo tawona mulwali kuti maso banu."

"Lazalo wati wapulika ivyo Soyaphi wakayowoyanga, mbwenu kumaso banu."

"Musungwana bakamuchichizga mpaka makongono banu."

Bazu

This comes from the verbs "kubazula" to break with force or to sever or "kubazuka" to be broken.

"*bazu*" is in reference to the actual breaking or separation of a piece from another piece.

"Mphika wati wawa pasi, mbwenu bazu."

Bendereske[2]

This is derived from the verb "kubendereska" to cause to bend or deform or to distort.

'*bendereske*' is the act of deforming or distorting or bending an object. If repeated, '*bendereske-bendereske*' is in reference to total distortion.

"Enya Lazalo kulima wali kulima, kweni mizele yose mbwenu dala bendereske/bendereske-bendereske."

Bendezge[2]

This is from the verb "kubendezga" to form a curve or cause to bend or to distort.

'*bendezge*' is in reference to the act of deforming, or distorting. If repeated, '*bendezge-bendezge*' it is in reference to continued acts of causing deformation.

"Chandiwira mumalo mwakunyoloska chisulo, mbwenu bendezge/bendezge-bendezge."

Beneku

This comes from the verb "kubenekula" to uncover e.g. taking off a lid or cover; or to open – as with a book.

'*beneku*' is in reference to that action of uncovering, or opening.

"Agogo ŵati ŵagona, mbwenu kazukulu bulangeti lawo lila beneku."

"Wati wageza mumawoko, mbwenu mbale ya sima yila beneku."

Beng'ende

'beng'ende' is in reference to being nude – or, simply, complete nakedness.

"Ŵankhungu ŵakamupoka malaya Tumbikani nakumuleka beng'ende."

Benu

This is from the verb "kubenula" to open (as with eyes or a book).

'benu' is in reference to opening.

"Kuti timanye kuti wachali wamoyo, mbwenu tasanga Mwiza maso benu."

Beteku[2]

This comes from the verb "kubetekula" to suddenly move with a swing or jolt without due concern.

'beteku' is in reference to the act of walking or moving in a jolt, or being barely clothed. If repeated, 'beteku-beteku' is in reference to continuous unconcerned jolting movements of one's body, or being poorly dressed as a result of poverty.

"Apo tikatenge takola kathole, mbwenu kathole kala beteku."

"Mwanakazi yula pakwenda wakuchita kuti beteku-beteku."

"Soni zikutikola – awonani mukamwana wakuchita kuti beteku-beteku pakwenda chifukwa cha ukavu."

Bewu

This is from the verbs "kubewula" to tilt or overturn, or "kubewuka" also to overturn or to suddenly arrive at home or village or place.

'bewu' is in reference to overturning or the sudden arrival or appearnce of someone not expected.

"Galimoto yikhateleleka mpaka bewu."

"Tembani wati wafika pamalo ghakutayira viswaswa, mbwenu galimoto yake bewu."

"Uko tikulindizga, mbwenu mulendo yula bewu."

Bibinyu[2]

This is derived from the verb "kubibinyuka" to stretch oneself as when in fatigue or in some body pain.

'bibinyu' is in reference to the act of stretching one's limbs or body. If repeated, *'bibinyu-bibinyu'* denotes several acts of stretching.

"Wati wendeska kamunwe pa muwongo wake, mbwenu mwana msana bibinyu/bibinyu-bibinyu."

Bilinkhinyu[2]

This comes from the verb "kubilinkhinyuka" to wriggle.

'bilinkhinyu' simply refers to the act of wriggling – like in the movement of muscles of a worm. In a derogatory sense, the idiophone can also be used to describe the movements of one who is heavy/and fat – more so – women. If repeated, *'bilimkhinyu-bilimkhinyu'* is in reference to continuous muscle movements as the object is moving.

"Thondo (a caterpillar) likuchita kuti bilinkhinyu pakwenda."

"Mandinda pala wakwenda, nyuma yose ni bilinkhinyu-bilinkhinyu."

Bilu

This comes from the verb "kubila" to sink, or to drown, or simply to go below the water surface.

'bilu' refers to the act of going below the water surface, or an object drowning.

"Uko tichali kuti tichiwoneske, mbwenu chigwele chila mu maji bilu."

Bing'inthu[2]

This comes from the verb "kubing'inthula" to move one's body muscles or bums provocatively.

'bing'inthu' is in reference to a single muscle movement. If repeated, *'bing'inthu-bing'inthu'* is in reference to repetitive muscle movements.

"Awonani linunda la nkhuzi likuchita kuti bing'inthu pala yikwenda."

"Phelire wakuchita kuti matako dala bing'inthu-bing'inthu pakwenda."

Bingizu-bingizu

This is derived from the noun "bingiza," the name of an insect heavy in build and clumsy in movement.

'bingizu-bingizu' refers to clumsy movements" as of that insect "bingiza."

"Amuwoneni Lazalo pakwenda bingizu-bingizu nga ni bingiza."

Binkhiske²

This stems from the verb "kubinkhiska" to dirten or to soil.

'binkhiske' refers to the act or action of soiling. If repeated, *'binkhiske-binkhiske'* denotes more than one stroke of smudging.

"Apo Lumbani wakawelanga kufuma ku sukulu, mbwenu malaya dala binkhiske."

"Wati wanjila mu mathipa, mbwenu malaya binkhiske-binkhiske."

Binyu²

This stems from the verb "kubinyuka" to draw one's spine inwards as when tickled, or to dance in wriggles – particularly along one's back and waist.

'binyu' is in reference to the motion of a wriggle – or that sudden reaction of the body from a tickle.

"Wati wamumuchilikita, mbwenu Soyaphi binyu/binyu-binyu."

"Mafunase wakuchita kuti binyu/binyu-binyu pa kuvina."

Bitiku

'bitiku' is in reference to size of a dress or skirt being too tight and short and exposing the thighs.

"Ŵasungwana madazi ghano pakuvwala ni bitiku."

Bitiku²

This is from the verb "kubitikula" to drum in short and fast rhythms

'bitiku-bitiku' is in reference to repeated drumming, but in short and fast rythms.

"Ng'oma yikapulikikwanga kuti bitiku-bitiku."

Boko

This stems from the verb "kubokola" to throw up, or to vomit.

'boko' is in reference to the gushing out of stuff, or a spurt.

"Mwana ŵakamukhapizga mpaka bala lose boko."

Bong'ontho

This is from the verb "kubong'onthola" also to dislodge an object from main.

'bong'ontho' refers to the dislodging.

"Thumbiko wakalimbana nalo jino mpaka bong'ontho."

Bontho

This comes from the verb "kubonthola" to break off a piece or a stem, or a leaf from a stem.

'bontho' refers to the separation of the object or leaf, or branch from the main stem.

"Uko Ulanda wakusuka komechi yake yadongo, mbwenu kakukolera bontho."

"Mwana wati wafika pa khuni la yembe, mbwenu mani bontho."

Bon'yo

This comes from the verb "kubon'yola" to dislodge a piece from the main – strictly speaking from something moulded or from gums.

'bon'yo' is in reference to the separation of the 'piece' from the main.

"Apo wakaseŵeleskanga komechi, mbwenu mwasoka kachikolelo bon'yo."

"Cheruzgo wakalimbana nalo jino mpaka bon'yo."

Bowo

This stems from the verbs "kubowola" to make a hole through a surface, or from the verb "kubowozga" to discover.

'bowo' is in reference to being through a surface – as with a needle through a piece of cloth, or an auger through a piece of wood. The ideophone can also be used when, after a long puzzle, a solution is suddenly found.

"Tikajima libwe mpaka bowo kuti tisange maji."

"Mhaŵi wati watilongosolera, mbwenu ziŵalo zikatitonda zila bowo."

Bugudu[2]

This comes from the verb "kubugudula" to search everywhere unsystematically.

'*bugudu*' or '*bugudu-bugudu*' is in reference to objects being thrown and banging against each other as the search is on.

"Kasi ndine pela nkhupulika kuti bugudu/bugudu-bugudu mu nyumba?"

Buli

This comes from the verb "kubulika" to suddenly pop-out from nowhere, or from underground.

'*buli*' is in reference to that sudden and unexpected appearance.

"Apo Songelwayo wakajimanga mbeŵa panthena apo, mbwenu mbeŵa zile buli pafupi na ise."

"Uko tikuchezga, mbwenu Phyoka nayo buli."

Bulukutu

'*bulukutu*' is in reference to something, or someone that looks heavily built, and without shape – simply like a drum.

"Uku nkhututuŵa kuwemwe chara – awonani mwana wachita kuti bulukutu."

Bwa

This is from the verb 'kubwaka' to entrap or to capture.

'*bwa*' is in reference to the act of entrapping, or capturing.

"Apo kayuni kati kaduke, mbwenu Soyaphi wali nako bwa."

Bwanganda

This is from the verbs "kubwangandula" to break apart, or to demolish, or "kubwanganduka" to be broken.

'*bwanganda*' is in reference to things falling apart.

"Nozgechi chikhazi wakaŵa nacho, kwene juzi lene apa mbwenu nthengwa bwanganda."

Bwanganda[2]

This comes from the verb "kubwangandula" to clang, or cause a loud metallic sound.

'bwanganda' is in reference to a single ringing of metallic sound as an object bangs against another. If repeated, *'bwanganda-bwanganda'* is in reference to continued clangs.

"Mumalo mwakuti wapenje mwakufwasa, mbwenu Lazalo mu nyuma bwanganda-bwanganda."

Bwankhu

This is derived from the verb "kubwankhula" to goad someone in the jaw so as to provoke.

'bwankhu' is in reference to the act of goading, or prodding into someone's face or chin/jaw.

"Kasi mungavipulika? Mzondi mwana muchoko yula mbwenu wali naye mukulu wake bwankhu!"

Bwanthu

This comes from the verb "kubwanthula" to lower or cause to move down – as in lowering a lifted roof of a grain store.

'bwanthu' refers to the action of letting go down. Could also be used as slang in reference to a fallen face – or the sudden drop of the head – as when dying.

"Tiyezge wati wamala kutola ngoma mu nthamba, mbwenu kaŵale yula bwanthu."

"Uku tikuchezga naye Soyaphi mu chipatala, mbwenu Soyaphi yula bwanthu."

Bwanyu

This is from the verb "kubwanyula" to poke into one's cheek with a forefinger so as to incite anger or humiliation.

'bwanyu' (as in "bwankhu") refers to the act of poking or goading or prodding someone's jaws.

"Kuti Khuzwayo wamukalipiske munyake, mbwenu wali naye mu matama bwanyu."

Bwatike

This comes from the verb "kubwatika" to place something like a pot on the stove, or on the ground, or simply to dump.

'bwatike' ordinarily refers to that action of placing a pot on the stove or an object on the ground. In slang, however, "bwatike" refers to that action of dumping something.

"Nyengoyawo wati wamukhizga mwana ku muwongo, mbwenu pasi bwatike."

"Tembani wanamusinjilo – wati watola, mbwenu mwana waŵene pakaya bwatike – iye uyo!

Bwefu

This is from the verb "kubwefula" to throw someone down.

'bwefu' is in reference to the act of falling to the ground.

"Mwana wakapulumuka kumusana mpaka pasi bwefu."

"Temwa wakatutuzgika mpaka pasi bwefu."

Bwetu-bwetu

This derives from the verb "kubwetula" ordinarily, to say something meaningless. Some other times, however, "kubwetula" means to suddenly and innocently disclose a secret to a third party – taking others by surprise.

'bwetu' is in reference to suddenly say something unexpected. If repeated, 'bwetu-bwetu' is in reference to saying something incessantly and about nothing.

"Uko tikuti makani ghachali muchindindi, mbwenu Lazalo pa muzinda bwetu."

"Chiukepo manyi nkhufuntha – apo wakhala ni bwetu-bwetu."

Bwi/bwitu

This comes from the verb "kubwita" to dip into something such as a sauce.

'bwi' or 'bwitu' is in reference to the act of dipping into the sauce.

"Wati wamenya sima, mbwenu mu dende bwi/bwitu."

Bwitu-bwitu

This comes from the verb "kubwituka" to glitter due to oil or fatty substance smeared on a surface, or added to a particular type of food.

'bwitubwitu' is in reference to the glitter of surface such as skin, or lips due to too much oil or fat applied on them, or the glitter of a fatty stew. Sometimes it is used as slang in reference to an appetizing body – particularly that of a woman.

"Mzondwase waphaka mafuta kumaso mpaka bwitu-bwitu."

"Siyenji madazi ghano wakuchita kuti bwitu-bwitu."

Byoko

This comes from the verb "kubyokola" to ejaculate.

'byoko' is in reference to squirting, or coming out of semen.

"Manyi ni matenda – Yezgani kuwona waka mwanakazi, mbwenu byoko."

Ŵaŵanu

This is from the verb "kuŵanula" or "kuŵaŵanula to forcibly separate two objects stuck together.

'ŵaŵanu' is in reference to the gradual separation, or opening, as force is being exerted.

"Visulo vyati vyakolana, tikachichizga mpaka visulo vila ŵaŵanu."

Ŵaje²

This comes from the verb 'kuŵaja' – to carve or to chip.

"ŵaje" or "ŵaje-ŵaje" is in reference to either a single act of carving or several acts of chipping.

"Soyaphi phesulo lamwene wali nalo ŵaje/ŵaje-ŵaje."

Ŵandu

This comes from the verb "kuŵandula" to split an object with force – as in splitting a log of wood.

'ŵandu' is in reference to the result – the occurrence of the split.

"Mbavi yikawa yakuthwa – kamoza na kamoza mbwenu thabwa bandu."

In slang, both the verb "kubandula" or the idiophone *"bandu"* can also be used in reference to the hard stinging of punches in a fight or a boxing match.

"Nanga uli Lazalo wakayezga kuti waŵeke, Soyaphi wali naye mumutu bandu."

Ŵangandu

This comes from the verb "kuŵangandula" to hit or beat severely.

'ŵangandu' is used in reference to the act of hard beating or clubbing.

"Uko Mzondi wakuti wachimbile, mbwenu nthonga mumutu ŵangandu."

Ŵawu

This is derived from the verb "kuŵaŵula" to scorch or to burn on the surface.

'ŵaŵu' is in reference to the passing of a heat wave over the skin and having it scorched just on the surface.

"Apo Chimwemwe wakayezganga kuzimwa moto, mbwenu mawoko ghose ŵaŵu."

Ŵeŵefu-ŵeŵefu

This is derived from the verb "kuŵeŵefuka" to pant or to be out of breath because of exertion.

'ŵeŵefu-ŵeŵefu'– is in reference to the act of panting, or fast breathing as a result of exertion.

"Awonani Tawina wakuchita kuti ŵeŵefu-ŵeŵefu chifukwa cha kuchimbira."

Ŵeku

This is from the verb "kuŵeka" to shield off, or to turn aside an advancing blow or weapon.

'ŵeku' is in reference to the act of shielding off, or diverting the onslaught using a shield or simply one's arms.

"Lazalo wati waponya mkondo, Soyaphi wali nawo ŵeku na chiskango."

Ŵenu[2]

This comes from the verb "kuŵenuka" to be yonder, or "kuŵenuska" to cause to go over and beyond.

'ŵenu' is in reference to the act of going over a challenge, as in high jump. If repeated *'ŵenu-ŵenu'* is in reference to going over or flying over towering heights.

"Dumisani wakatimba bola mpaka nyumba ŵenu."

"Nombo yikaduka mpaka mapili ghose ŵenu-ŵenu."

Ŵewu

This is from the verb "kuŵewula" or "kuŵeŵuka" to hive off (as with grass thatch) or to be hived off.

'ŵewu' is in reference to grass thatch being hived off or lifted off.

"Kavuluvulu wakiza nankhongono mpaka utheka pa nyumba ŵewu."

Ŵindu[2]

This stems from the noun "kaŵindu-ŵindu" – a water spring – or in slang – "chaos" or "confusion."

'ŵindu' – is in reference to a single stroke of a stir or stimulation. If repeated, 'ŵindu-ŵindu' is in reference to a continous stir, or continuous stimulation – as in the movement of water at a spring or the coming on of nausea, emotions, spread of cancer or, in the atmosphere – the movement of clouds.

"Wati waponyamo libwe la moto mu chipindi, mbwenu phele ŵindu/ŵindu-ŵindu."

"Masozi wati wamwa mankhwala, mbwenu chikoso cha kufuma nacho ŵindu."

"Muhanya uno kundache makola yayi – kuchanya kukuchita kuti ŵindu-ŵindu."

ŵiru-ŵiru

This comes from the verb "kuŵira" – to come to boil.

'ŵiruŵiru' is in reference to the movement of water in a pot as it is beginning to boil.

"Maji pamoto ghambapo sono kuti ŵiruŵiru."

Ŵisu

This is derived from the verb "kuŵisula"or "kuŵisuka" to make a facial expression that displays vanity, or contempt.

'ŵisu' is in reference to the act of grimacing depicting vanity or contempt.

"Chimango wakuchita kuti ŵisu pakutilaŵiska chifukwa cha malaya ghasono agho wavwala."

Ŵitu[2]

This is from the verb "kuŵitula" to jerk one's tail – as with a bird, or a costume, or bums.

'ŵitu' is in reference to a single jerk of one's tail, or costume, or bum. If repeated, 'ŵitu-ŵitu' is in reference to a series of such movements.

"Mwakawona ka kathyethye mchila ŵitu/ŵitu-ŵitu."

"Pala Lusungu wakuvina, malaya nagho ni ŵitu."

Chakamu[2]

This comes from the verb "kuchakamula" to chew.

'chakamu' refers to the act of chewing or munching. If repeated, 'chakamu-chakamu' is in reference to continuous chewing.

"Thumbiko wati ponye skawa mu mulomo, mbwenu chakamu/chakamu-chakamu."

Chali (also see "tyali")

'chali' is in reference to the coming out of squirts of fluid or liquid in small quantities – e.g. in the last stage of urination.

"Nanga uli wakayezga kukhwinyilizga, mbwenu paumalilo tawona munthu matuzi chali."

Chanthu

This comes from the verb "kuchantha" to become sour in taste or emotion.

'chanthu' is in reference to the feel in the mouth of a sharp and sour taste – as in milk gone bad, or in the taste of lemon.

"Wati wawulaŵa moŵa, wakasanga kuti uli chanthu."

"Mumukole makola Nthembozawo – pala wali pala wali chanthu."

Chegedu

This comes from the verb "kuchegedula" to brutally break someone's skin – ordinarily through use of fingernails.

'chegedu' is in reference to the sudden opening of the skin.

"Apo ŵakasinananga, Lazalo wali naye Suzgo chegedu pa kawoko."

Cheketu

This comes from the verb "kucheketa" to cut or to sever.

"*cheketu*' is in reference to cutting or severing.

"Salu yaŵene, mbwenu Lazalo wali nayo cheketu."

"Chakufwa wati wakola nkhuku, mbwenu singo cheketu."

Cheleru

This comes from the verb "kuchelera" to be early.

'*cheleru*' refers to the act of taking off very early, or starting something before the expected or usual time.

"Chimango wati wapulika za yifwa ku Boma, mbwenu kumachero kwake cheleru."

Chengachenga

This comes from the verb "kuchengachenga" to be restless or scared of the unknown.

'*chengachenga*' is in reference to acts of discomfort or uneasiness due to fear of the unknown – as in a convict waiting for sentencing or in a thief caught redhanded.

"Wati wawona ŵasilikali, mbwenu Chiphwafu chengachenga."

Chenu

This is from the verb "kuchenuka" to suddenly look behind.

'*chenu*' is in reference to the act of quickly looking behind often in response to a prod or some signal.

"Wati wapulika kuswaya kunyuma, mbwenu Soyaphi chenu."

"Wati wakhwasika pa phewa, mbwenu Fumbani chenu."

Chenye[2]

This comes from the verb "kuchenya" to rebuke or scold sternly.

'*chenye*' is in reference to the act of rebuking or scolding. If repeated, '*chenye-chenye*' is in reference to a thorough rebuke.

"Womama ŵati ŵamukhazika pasi Tapiwa, ŵali naye chenye/chenye-chenye."

Cherezgu

This comes from the verb "kucherezga" to initiate action earlier than expected.

'cherezgu' is in reference to the act of starting something too early – like harvesting a crop when it is not ready.

"Apo ŵanyamata ŵakenelanga kwamba nchito pa nyengo yimoza, mbwenu Yotamu nchito yila cherezgu!"

Chete/chetee

These stem from the verb "kuchetama" to be silent, or quiet.

'chete' is is in reference to being quiet, wheras *'chetee'* is in reference to reflection in silence.

"Musambizgi wati wanjila mu kalasi, mbwenu ŵana chete."

"Madoda ghati ghamususya, mbwenu Yezgani chetee."

Chewu[2]

This is from the verb "kuchewula" to beckon – or to summon one's attention through a beckon.

'chewu' is in reference to the act of beckoning. If repeated, *"chewu-chewu'* is in reference either to continuous beconing, or continuous turning of one's head from left to right – as when uncertain to the direction of the source of sound or distraction.

"Mukachetechete, mbwenu Tafwakose wali naye Masozi chewu."

"Tikati tizelezge uli kwali, mbwenu Maria umo wambila chewu-chewu" kwa taŵanyake.

"Manyi ni mantha – awonani Chiphwafu apo wakhala wali chewu-chewu."

Chilikitu

This is from the verb "kuchilikita" to tickle.

'chilikitu' is in reference to the act of tickling.

"Wati wadekha Tawina, Lazalo wali naye munkhwapa chilikitu."

Chilu

This is from the verbs "kuchiluka" to be disturbed or to be alarmed, or "kuchiluska" to alarm.

'*chilu*' is in reference to the body reaction – as when tickled, or alarmed, or confronted when not ready.

"Chifukwa cha chiwawa, mbwenu mwana uyo wakagonanga chilu."

"Wati wamanya kuti muwoli wake ni fwiti, mbwenu Nyamazawo chilu."

Chinge[2]

This is from the verb "kuchinga" to stand firm in (a) protecting something, or a position or (b) taking an unwavering position on a point of argument.

'*chinge*' is in reference to the act of protecting. If repeated, '*chinge-chinge*' is in reference to total closure of loopholes, or weak links in a given situation.

"Madoda ghati ghawona kuti kukwiza ŵalwani, mbwenu chikaya chila chinge na minkhwala."

"Lazalo na Soyaphi ŵachita kuti chinge-chinge minda yawo na makuni gha minga."

Chinthu (also see "chilu")

This is derived from the verb "kuchinthuka" to be startled.

'*chinthu*' is the act of being startled, or the reaction to being startled.

"Soyaphi wati wamukola Maria mu chiuno, mbwenu Maria chinthu."

Chitunutunu

'*chitunutunu*' is in reference to the act of walking backwards as a result of some pressure or fear.

"Wanangwa wakawelela chitunutunu wati wawona vyaminthondwe."

Chokonyu

This comes from the verb "kuchokonya" to poke with something sharp – as in picking one's gums – or as in prodding a snake in its hiding place.

'*chokonyu*' referes to the act of poking or prodding.

"Njoka yati yanjila ku khululu, mbwenu Mzondi wali nayo chokonyu na kakhuni."

Chotopu (also see "sotopu")

This comes from the verbs "kuchotopola" or "kuchotoposka" to flush out game or a person from some comfort zone.

'chotopu' is in reference to the act of suddenly jumping out of hiding, or the act of suddenly leaving a comfort zone.

"Timeyo wati wayichiluska nyiska, mbwenu nyiska yila chotopu."

"Chananga wati wawona kuti pakaya pakhala uheni, mbwenu ku usiku chotopu."

Chu-chu-chu

This is from the verb "kuchucha" to leak.

'chu-chu-chu' is in reference to a voluminous leak – as with rain through a roof, or puss from a wound.

"Vula yati yawa, mbwenu maji mu nyumba chu-chu-chu."

"Chitufya chati chaphulika, mafira ghakachita kuti chu-chu-chu."

Chumbululu

This is from the verbs "kuchumbuluka" to be watery, or "kuchumbuluska" to dilute – as in preparation of porridge or in dilution of paint.

'chumbululu' is in reference to the light texture of liqiud – as in soup, porridge, or traditional brews, etc.

'Manyi ufu ukaŵa uchoko, bala likachita kuti chumbululu."

Chumbuluske

This is also from the verb "kuchumbuluska" to dilute, or make a liquid less concentrated – especially by adding more water or a thiner.

'chumbuluske' is in reference to the act of diluting, or causing dilution.

"Nanga uli Uchizi ŵakamuphalila kuti bala likhome, iye mbwenu dala chumbuluske."

Chunkhu

This comes from the verb "kuchunkhuska" to scare off a crowd of animals, birds, or people and cause them to run into all directions.

'chunkhu' is in reference to the act of animals, or birds, or people scattering into all directions because of being scared.

"Njoka yati yawa pakati pawo, mbwenu ŵanthu ŵose chunkhu."

"Chunkhuske²

This is also from the verb "kuchunkhuska" to cause to scatter, or cause to disperse – as in a crowd.

'chunkhuske' is in reference to the act of dispersing, or scattering. Also see "chunkhu."

"Chimbwe wati wanjila mu chiŵaya, mbwenu mbuzi chunkhuske/chunkhuske-chunkhuske."

Chupu

This is derived from the verb "kuchupula" to swoop down and brush over a target – as an eagle skimming over a prey.

'chupu' is in reference to the sudden brush, or contact between the aggressor and the prey and in the process raising lots of dust. Sometimes it is in reference to the act of hit and run.

"Apo nkhuku yikalyanga, Luhera wali nato twana chupu."

"Apo Yezgani wakati wajumphe musewu, mbwenu galimoto yili naye chupu."

Chuu

This is from the verb "kuchuluska" to over-fill, or to fill beyond capacity, or have too much – as in too much food on a plate, or too much money.

'chuu' is in reference to too much in terms of quantity.

"Lazalo wakawina vindalama chuu."

Daa

'daa' is in reference to a quiet liquid surface – especially water – being calm and clear – as in a lake, or the sky.

"Nyanja yachita kuti daa."

"Usange msuni/msuzi uli daa, ndiko kuti mama watondeka kuphika dende."

Dakwi²

This is from the verb "kudakwira" to gasp – as in someone being choked.

'dakwi' is in reference to the act of a single gasp. If repeated, *'dakwi-dakwi'* is in reference to continued acts of gasping.

"Awonani somba dakwi/dakwi-dakwi chifukwa chakuyifumiska mu maji."

Dapi

This is from the verbs "kudapila" to shun from truth – or to avoid truth – or from the verb "kudapilana" – to pass on blame to one another.

'dapi' is in reference to the act of shunning from truth.

"Soyaphi wati wamupanikizga Lazalo naunenesko, mbwenu Lazalo dapi."

Dekezge

This is from the verb "kudekezga" to perch and balance an object on the head, or bend one's neck.

'dekezge' is the act of balancing the object on one's head, or bending one's neck.

"Wati wateka maji, mbwenu Maria msuku wake pa mutu dekezge."

"Mwamuwona Mwiza pakwenda – wakuchita kuti singo dekezge!"

Dekhe (also see "fwase")

This is from the verb "kudekha" to be oblivious to one's surrounding environment.

'dekhe' is in reference to the act of being unaware of one's surroundings – as with a monkey completely absorbed in eating and totally unaware of lurking danger.

Chifukwa cha matyokolo, mbwenu munkhwele dekhe."

Delu²

This comes from the verb "kudeluka" to go past one's sight, or vision in a flash – as in a racing car driving past.

'delu' is in reference to the sudden, and fast movement of an object across one's vision. If repeated, *'deludelu'* is in reference to repeated flashes of movements across one's sight.

"Namunyinu ndawona muntu apa delu – kasi ndi njani?"

"Mwaŵana mwamba mbele deludelu pa madoda – kasi mulije nchindi?"

Denyu²

This comes from the verb "kudenya" to jiggle, or to dance in short jerky movements.

'denyu' is in reference to a single jerky movement in a jig or dance.

"Ng'oma zati zamba kwimba, mbwenu mwana nayo wamba denyu/denyu-denyu."

Didimizge²

This comes from the verb "kudidimizga" to emphasize, or to push an object under water, fluid or surface.

'didimizge' is in reference to the act of emphasizing or pushing some object under surface.

"Madoda ghati ghachetama mbwenu Lazalo fundo yake yila didimizge/didimizge-didimizge kuti ŵapulikiske."

"Kulongola kuti mwana ŵakumuzomelezga mu mpingo, mbwenu mwana yula mu maji didimizge."

Dikimu

This stems from the verb "kudikimula" to hit severely using a stick.

'dikimu' is in reference to the act of hitting.

"Apo wakati wathaŵe, Khuzwayo wali naye dikimu Tembani na mubada."

Diku²

This comes from the verb "kudikula" to gyrate – as in a sexual act.

'diku' is in reference to a single movement of gyrating. If repeated, *'diku-diku'* is in reference to continuous acts of gyrating.

"Ncheŵe yati yakwela yinyake, mbwenu diku/diku-diku."

Dininizge²

This is from the verb 'kudininizga' to press hard so as to leave a mark or impression.

'dininizge' is in reference to the act of pressing hard on some object. If repeated, *'dininizge-dininizge'* is in reference to either acts of pressing on several objects, or a single thorough act.

"Tati taŵika kapepala pachanya pa ndalama ya njawala, mbwenu dininizge/dininizge-dininizge kuti tifumizge chithuzi."

"Tati tapanda makuni, mbwenu mumphepete mwa khuni lili lose dininizge-dininizge kuti likhole."

Dirimu

This comes from the verbs "kudirimula" to pull down – as with a wall, or "kudirimuka" to collapse, or slide down – also as with a wall, or as in a land slide.

'*dirimu*' is in reference to the falling of the columns or the sliding of the mass into some heap.

"Kuwa kwa vula kula, mbwenu chiliŵa chose dirimu."

Dirizu

This comes from the verb "kudiriza" or "kudirizula" to rip, or tear away someone's skin – as when playing soccer.

'*dirizu*' is in reference to the act of ripping or tearing the skin away.

"Palichi wakamugulumula mwa nkhaza mwana mpaka pa musana dirizu."

Diwidiwi

'*diwidiwi*' is in refererence to people's heads being lowered – as in mourning – depicting a gloomy atmosphere.

"Apo tikafikanga pa yifwa, ŵanthu ŵose ŵakaŵa diwidiwi."

Do-do-do

This is from the verb "kudodomela" to sink – as in a boat sinking.

'*do-do-do*' is in reference to the motion of sinking.

"Maji ghati ghazula mu wato, nakalinga mbwenu wato do-do-do."

Dodoli

This is from the verb "kudodoliska" to stare without a blink.

'*dodoli*' is in reference to an unflinching stare.

"Mwana wakanilaŵiska dodoli."

Domadoma

'*domadoma*' is in reference to the act of approaching a target without hesitation or flinching.

"Apo nkhayezganga kumuwofyeza Mayengiso na nthonga, mbwenu iye domadoma."

Domo (also see "donyo," "doso")

This is from the verb "kudomola" to cut off – as with a string.

'*domo*' is in reference to the severing.

"Lazalo na Soyaphi ŵakaguzana mpaka chingwe domo."

Donyo

This comes from the verb "kudonyola" to cut off.

'*donyo*' is in reference to the cutting off.

"Wati waguza chingwe, mbwenu chingwe chila donyo."

"Wati wamalizga kujovwila, mbwenu kamchimba donyo."

Donyorezge

This is from the verb "kudonyorezga" to stop completing a process.

'*donyorezge*' is in reference to the act of halting, or bringing to a stop unexpectedly.

"Suzgika wati wachiluskika, mbwenu kurya donyorezge."

Doso

This is from the verb "kudosola" to separate a piece by pulling it off the main – e.g. a piece of rope from a coil, or a piece of thread from a reel.

'*doso*' is in reference to the snapping, or the separation from the main as a result of pulling.

"Kondwani wakaguza nkhwamba mpaka doso."

Du (also see "nu")

'*du*' is in reference to being silent, or not responding – as in a person being interrogated but not responding.

"Tafwakose wakayezga kuti wamuyowoyeske Masozi, kweni munyake mbwenu du."

Dukuma or Dukumale

This comes from the verb "kudukumala" to squat as in a crouch.

'dukuma' or *'dukumale'* is in reference to sitting or squatting with the knees bent and shoulders drawn inwards.

"Mwamuwona Dumisani umo wakhalila pakati pa madoda – wati waka dukuma/dukumale."

Dunde[2]

This is from the verb "kudunda" to sulk or to be sullen.

'dunde' is in reference to sulking. If repeated, *'dunde-dunde'* is in reference to complete sullenness either in a single individual or several persons.

"Duti wati wamuchenya Maria, mbwenu mwana yula dunde."

"Tati tanjila mu nthanganeni, mbwenu ŵasungwana wose dunde-dunde."

Dunduzu

This comes from the verb "kudunduzula" to bounce an object against the ground.

'dunduzu' is in reference to the bouncing of the object against the ground.

"Soyaphi wakamukanchizga munyake mpaka pasi dunduzu."

Dupu

This comes from the verb "kudupula" to whip.

'dupu' is in reference to the act of whipping.

"Lazalo wati watola mchiza, mbwenu mwa Soyaphi dupu."

Dweku

This is from the verb "kudwekula" to throw someone off balance onto the ground.

'dweku' is in reference to the act of awkwardly falling to the ground as a result of being thrown off.

"Wanangwa ŵakamukung'untha mpaka wakawa uko dweku."

Dyakamu

This comes form the verb "kudyaka" or "kudyakamula" – to step on, or to beat severely.

'*dyakamu*' is in reference to that act of stepping on something, or beating severely.

"Apo nkhati nimujumphe, mbwenu wali nane dyakamu pakalundi kuwezgzela nduzga."

"Apo wakati wachimbile Mopho, mbwenu Tifapi wali naye dyakamu mu msana na musi."

Dyamphanthu

This is from the verb "kudyamphanthuka" to be drenched to the skin.

'*dyamphanthu*' is in reference to being drenched and dripping.

"Mazaza vula yikamutimba mpaka iye na malaya dyamphanthu."

Dyamu

This is from the verb "kudyamula" also to beat severely.

'*dyamu*' is in reference to beating or thomping.

"Tati takola waka mnkhungu yula, mbwenu naye dyamu."

Dyelewu[2]

This comes from the verb "kudyelewuka" to be slimy, or slippery – as in derere or okra.

'*dyelewu*' is in reference to the feel of slime – and if repeated, '*dyelewu-dyelewu*' is in reference to a repeated, or continuous feel of slime – as in the texture of delele or okra.

"Delele lati lapya, likachita kuti dyelewu/dyelewu-dyelewu pakulya."

Dyonkho

This comes from the verb "kudyonkhola" to off-load a heavy object to the ground usually from the shoulder, or from the head – as with a bundle of firewood.

'*dyonkho*' is in reference to the fall, or landing to the ground of the object.

"Wati wafika pa kaya, mbwenu Nyembezi mtolo wake wa nkhuni pasi dyonkho."

"Phyoka wakakhuŵala mpaka pasi dyonkho."

Dyu-dyu-dyu

'dyu-dyu-dyu' is in reference to the act of systematically forcing an object into a narrow wet space – and in the process causing some friction.

"Wongani wati watola chigamu, mbwenu mu botolo la maji dyu-dyu-dyu."

Dyuku (also see "thibu")

This is from the verb "kudyukula" to pound to powder, or to pulp.

'dyuku' is thus in reference to the hard contact with the object being pounded, or being hit.

"Ŵalyenge wati watola musi, mbwenu gaga wake dyuku mu thuli."

Fike

This is from the verb "kufika" to arrive.

'fike' is in reference to arriving.

"Uko tichali zina-zina, mbwenu mulwani fike."

Finyikizge

This is from the verb "kufinyikizga" to squeeze into some narrow space.

'finyikizge' is in reference to the squeezing of oneself into a narrow space.

"Tamala wati wawona kuti malo ghakukhala ghamala, mbwenu pakati pa ŵanyake finyikizge."

Fiske[2]

This is from the verb "kufiska" either to meet one's obligation, or target or duty, or to deliver a message.

'fiske' is in reference to the act of finalising. If repeated, *'fiske-fiske'* is reference to all obligations being met, or completing all that had been set out.

"Nanga uli Gomezgani ŵakamutangwaniskanga, nchito yose iyo wakapika mbwenu fiske/fiske-fiske."

"Wati wafika, mbwenu Lazalo makani agho wakatumika fiske/fiske-fiske ku madoda."

Fongo

This is from the verb "kufongola" to stoop and expose one's buttocks, or anus.

'fongo' is in reference to that posture of one stooping and exposing one's behind or anus.

"Kasi Soyaphi nkhukhala kuweme uko kuchita kuti fongo pakati pa muzinda?"

Fote[2]

This is from the verb "kufota" to wilt.

'fote' is in reference to wilting. If repeated, *'fote-fote'* is in reference to wilting in a large scale.

"Mtika wati wamala, mbwenu mahamba nagho fote/fote-fote."

Fukafuka

This comes from the verb "kufukafuka" to strive relentlessly for something.

'fukafuka' is in reference to the act of restless search for something.

"Apo ise tikatenge kuwalo kulichi, munyithu Chandiwira mbwenu fukafuka kunozgekela kwiza kwa vula."

Fukatile

This comes from the verb "kufukatila" to engulf for protection – as in placing a child in the lap, or to comfort someone – as when in mourning.

'fukatile' is in reference to the act of protecting someone from discomfort, or the act of comforting someone.

"Chigomezgo wati wapima, mbwenu nyina wake wali naye fukatile."

"Munyithu wati wafelwa, mbwenu chikaya chose munyithu yula fukatile."

Fuku/Fukule[2]

This comes from the verb "kufukula" to remove soil from a trough or hole.

'fuku' or *'fukule'* is in reference to that act of scooping loose soil from a trough or hole.

"Tati tawezgeramo dongo mu khululu, mbwenu Chiphwafu dongo lila fuku kupenja mphiyi."

Chiukepo wati wajimajima, mbwenu dongo lila fukule/fukule-fukule."

Fukumale (also see "dukumale")

This comes from the verb "kufukumala" to crouch or to bend low with legs and body close.

'fukumale' is in reference either to positioning oneself into a crouch – either in a sitting position or when asleep.

"Munthu uyo wati fukumale apo, ndiyo mweneyuyo tikupenja."

Fukunyu

This comes from the verb "kufukunyula" – to rummage through a collection of things, or to frisk.

'fukunyu' is in reference to the act of rummaging through a collection of things and exposing concealed objects. Could also be used in reference to the act of probing into one's privacy, etc.

"Lazalo wali nalo thumba la Mazaza fukunya kupenja ndalama yake iyo yikazgewa."

"Makani agho tikabisa, mbwenu Mopho wati wafika, makhani ghala fukunyu."

Fukunyule[2]

This is also from the verb "kufukunyula" to delve into a container and scatter out its contents – as in pulling out contents of a pillow or a suitcase, or as in an investigation.

'fukunyule' is in reference to the act of delving and scattering, or spilling out contents. If repeated, *'fukunyule-fukunyule'* is in reference to continued rummaging and leaving contents scattered all over.

"Tati tajula maputumeti, mbwenu ŵa silikali malaya ghithu fukunyule/fukunyule-fukunyule kupenja katundu uyo wakibika."

Fukutu-fukutu

This is from the verb "kufukutuka" to disintegrate, or to break into powder as a result of rot or dryness.

'fukutu-fukutu' is in reference to the disintegration, or breaking of substance into fragments (could be food or a piece of wood) due to rot.

"Nyama yakwanika, pakulya ni fukutu-fukutu."

Fulufulu

'*fulufulu*' is in reference to the sudden upheaval of matter – as in an over flow.

"Sima yati yamba kubwata, mbwenu fulufulu mu nkhali."

"Ng'ombe yikafyenyeka mpaka mavi fulufulu."

Fulukutu[2]

This comes from the verb "kufulukuta" to be restless, particularly in bed.

'*fulukutu*' is in reference to a single movement of restlessness. If repeated '*fulukutu-fulukutu*" is in reference to continuous movements of limbs either while asleep, or once seated in a chair – and often to someone's irritation nearby.

"Chigomezgo usange wagona pela, mbwenu ni fulukutu/fulukutu-fulukutu."

Funchike

This is from the verb "kufunchika" to leave or to dump.

'*funchike*' is the act of dumping.

"Khetase wati wawona kuti wovwili wa mwana palive, mbwenu mwana yula kunchito kwa a wiske funchike."

Funthu[2]

This comes from the verb "kufunthula" to scatter soil usually with the use of one's foot.

'*funthu*' is in reference to a single act of scattering soil, or a collection of objects using one's foot. If repeated '*funthu-funthu*' is in reference to several such movements.

"Muwuso wati wafika mu munda umo tikalimamo skawa, mbwenu mizele funthu/funthu-funthu kupenja skawa izo zikakhalila pasi."

Furumu

This is from the verb "kufurumuka" to gush out – as with intestines.

'*furmu*' is in reference to the gushing out of some matter – as from a stomach.

"Soyaphi wakayiganda ncheŵe na galimoto mpaka matumbo ghose furumu."

Futumu

This is derived from the verb "kufutumula" to turn inside out – as with a pocket.

'futumu' is in reference to the turning out of a pocket, or a bag.

"Muwuso kulongola kuti wandibe, mbwenu mathumba ghake ghose futumu."

Futupu

This comes from the verb "kufutupuska" to cause an object run out suddenly from a hiding place.

'futupu' is in reference to that sudden or unintended jump from a hiding place because of some scare.

"Nyiska yati yapulika kuswaya, mbwenu futupu."

Futwe-futwe

This is from the verb "kufutwa" to get weeviled – as in grain or in dried wood.

'futwe-futwe' is in reference to complete decay of grain, or wood because of termites or sheer dryness.

"Tisungane wati wavilikelela vingoma mu mathumba mbwenu vyose futwe-futwe."

Fuu

This comes from the verbs "kufunda" to warm up or "kufundiska" to heat up.

'fuu' is in reference to that feeling of warming, or heating up.

"Ŵanganya, munthu uyu wachali wa moyo – munkhwapa mwake muchali fuu."

Fuzufuzu

This is derived from the verb "kufuza" to spill out of a container because of heat – as in heated milk, or heated beer.

'fuzufuzu' is in reference to the effervescence and the spill out.

"Mukaka wati gaduke waka, mbwenu fuzufuzu."

Fwa[3]

This is in reference to being full – as with a container, or a river.

If said three times *'fwa-fwa-fwa'* is in reference to a container or a river being full to the brim, and spilling.

"Chidundu chazula fwa na ngoma."

"Vula yati yamala, dambo likachita kuti fwa-fwa-fwa."

Fwafwalala

'fwafwalala' is in reference to the act of falling over (induced or not induced) as a result of being physically weak.

"Muzukulu wawo wati waŵakanchizga agogo ŵakawa uko fwafwalala."

Fwagada (also see "fwigidu")

This comes from the verb "kufwagadula" to expose one's inner-self without due care.

'fwagada' is in reference to the act of opening or exposing one's inner thighs.

"Musungwana tikamusangilila wati fwagada pa mphasa."

Fwamphu

This comes from the verb "kufwamphula" to release a catch in a trap.

'fwamphu' is in reference to that sudden release of force – as in a trap released.

"Munkhwele wati wakhwaska msampha, mbwenu msampha ula fwamphu."

Fwanthamphu

This comes from the verb "kufwanthamphula" (as in "kufwamphula") to suddenly release a catch.

'fwanthamphu' as in *'fwamphu'* is in reference to the sudden release of a catch, particularly from a trap.

"Apo Cheruzgo wakati wabise makola msampha, wakachulukila msampha fwanthamphu."

Fwapu[2]

This is from the verb "kufwapuka" to over-fill as with water in a river, or to come out in abundance over some surface – as in a case of small pox, or mushrooms from the ground.

'fwapu' is in reference to either filling up, or the sudden appearance of something over skin or surface – such as a rash or soles on one's skin. If repeated, *'fwapu-fwapu'*, is in reference to the intensity of or spread of fluid or rash.

"Uchizi wakathila maji mu botolo mpaka fwapu."

"Mwana uyu walwala – awonani vilonda vyachita kuti fwapu ku mulomo."

"Zililo wati waphaka nkhama, mbwenu nthomba fwapu-fwapu mu thupi lose."

"Maji ghachita kuti fwapu-fwapu mu Rukuru umo vula yili kwambila."

Fwase[2]

This is from the verb "kufwasa" to be in a state of oblivion, or in a state of no concern and totally unaware of surroundings. On the other hand, the verb could allude to a state of tranquility in behaviour.

'fwase' is in reference to that act of being in oblivion or of being unaware of anything. If repeated, *'fwase-fwase'* is in reference to being in total oblivion or total tranquility.

"Ŵati ŵamala kulya vipaso, mbwenu ŵamunkhwele fwase/fwase-fwase."

"Wati watengwa Nozgechi, mbwenu mwana yula fwase/fwase-fwase – nga niyula wakasuzganga chala."

Fwatafwata/Fwatata

'fwatafwata' is in reference to the process of something deflating. It can also be in reference to one's inability to put up a strong or convincing argument.

"Bola lati lagwazika na munga, mbwenu fwatafwata/fwatata."

"Ŵati ŵamukunga na mafumbo, Soyaphi kuti wazgole mbwenu fwatata."

Fwatapu

This comes from the verb "kufwatapuska" to cause something to run out of hiding.

'fwatapu' is in reference to an animal's sudden jump – usually from resting or from hiding caused by some scare. Can also be used in reference to an unexpected rise from bed of a bed-ridden person.

"Nyiska yati yapulika kubwentha kwa ncheŵe, mbwenu fwatapu."

"Ng'anga yati yaluta, mbwenu Tamandenji nayo pa mphasa fwatapu."

Fwatu

This comes from the verb "kufwatula" to untie – as in a knot, or to release – as in a person in jail.

'fwatu' is in reference to that sudden looseness of a knot, or the unlocking of handcuffs. Can also be used where suddenly in a puzzle or an argument or a case, a solution is found.

"Temwanani mukulimbalimba, wakasanga nyozi zila ŵakamukaka nazo, fwatu."

"Wati waghanaghana nyengo yitali, mbwenu suzgo lila wakaŵa nalo, fwatu."

Fwelefwetu

This is from the verb "kufwelefwetuka" also to come out of resting – as with an animal.

'fwelefwetu' is in reference to the slow but steady rise of an animal from resting or slumber. Could also be used for humans – as they wake up from sleep.

"Dazi lati lamba kocha, mbwenu njati yila fwelefwetu."

"Tulo twati twamala, mbwenu Nyamazawo fwelefwetu pa mphasa."

Fwidigu/Fwidibu

These come from the verb "kufwidigula" or "kufwidibula" to expose the insides of the lips.

'fwidigu' or *'fwidibu'* is in reference to the act of showing the inside of lips or muscles.

"Kuti walongole sing'anga suzgo lake, mbwenu Chimango milomo yake fwidigu/fwidibu."

Fwinde[2]

This is derived from the verb "kufwinda" to jam, or fill a small space with something large, or to pack tightly into a confined space, or hole.

'fwinde' is in reference to the action of forcing something into a narrow space, or packing to capacity. If repeated, *'fwinde-fwinde'* is in reference to acts of continued jam-packing that leave no room whatsoever.

"Yakobe wati watola chigamu, wali nacho mu botolo fwinde."

"Nchindi wati watola dongo, mbwenu fwinde-fwinde mu ming'anya yose ya nyumba."

Fwinkhu[2]

This comes from the verbs "kufwinkha" to sniff repeatedly – as when sobbing or as when one tries to stop a running nose or "kufwinkhula" to snifle.

'fwinkhu' or *'fwinkhu-fwinkhu'* is in reference to the sniffs as one sobs or tries to control a running nose.

"Apo wakhala Nthembozawo ni fwinkhu/fwinkhu-fwinkhu chifukwa cha chitima."

Fwinthu (see "funthu")

This comes from the verb "kufwinthula" to scatter soil in a ridge using one's foot.

'fwinthu' refers to the act of stirring or scattering of soil particles.

"Apo Chigomezgo wakati fwinthu pa mizere, mbwenu skawa bweka-bweka."

Fwizu

This comes from the verb "kufwizula" to fall to the ground nose first or, in slang, to eat dust.

'fwizu' is in reference to the act of nose diving into hard ground – and in the process the nose getting bruised or covered in soil.

"Chigomezgo pakuwa, wakafikila mulomo fwizu mu dongo."

Fya or Fyati or Fyatike

These come from the verb "kufyatika" to place something in a confined space or gap.

'fya' or *'fyati'* or *'fyatike'* is in reference to that act of placing something in a confined space.

"Mukukhumba kubisa, mbwenu Takondwa ndalama yake pa lumwa la chiliŵa fya/fyati/fyatike.

"Wati wiba Ndalama, mbwenu mu nkhwapa fyatike."

Fyagadu/Fyakatu

This comes from the verb "kufyagadula" or "kufyakatula" to maliciously step on someone's foot or object with the intent to bruise or harm.

'fyagadu' or *'fyakatu'* is in reference to the brutal stepping onto an object with intent to bruise.

"Apo Lazalo na Mhaŵi ŵakazgalanga bola, mbwenu Soyaphi wali naye Lazalo fyagadu/fyakatu pa kalundi."

Fyapu (also see "thyapu")

This comes from the verb "kufyapula" to whip, or to beat mercilessly.

'fyapu' is in reference to the act of whipping, or thomping.

"Nchawaka uko wakuti wachimbile, Soyaphi wali nayo fyapu na liswazo."

Fyatile²

This is from the verb "kufyatila" to quickly hide something in the palm without being observed.

'fyatile' is in reference to the act of getting or receiving something and quickly hiding it in the palm.

"Ndati ndamupa kopala lake, mbwenu Dokiso kopala lila fyatile."

Fyee

This comes from the verb "kufyenya" to squeeze.

'fyee' is in reference to the act of squeezing.

"Mzondi pakukolana chasa, wakuchita kuti fyee kawoko kamunyake."

Fyekeze²

This comes from the verb "kufyekeza" to taunt, or to tease with jeers.

'fyekeze' is in reference to the act of taunting.

"Ŵasepuka ŵati ŵamusanga Tiwonge, mbwenu musungwana yula fyekeze/fyekeze-fyekeze mpaka koto!"

Fyenye² (also see "fyee")

Also from the verb "kufyenya" to squeeze.

'fyenye' is in reference to a single process of squeezing. If repeated, *'fyenye-fyenye'* is in reference to several squeezes, or several compressions.

"Phelile wati wamala kusukuluzga malaya, mbwenu malaya ghala fyenye/fyenye-fyenye kuti wakamuske maji."

Fyenyerezge[2]

This is from the verb "kufyenyerezga" to compress, or to squeeze hard, or, in slang, to oppress.

'fyenyerezge' is in reference to the squeeze or exertion so as to deny free movement, or the opportunity to rise above self.

"Nanga uli putumeti yikaŵa yichoko, mbwenu Chimwemwe malaya ghose fyenye-rezge/fyenyerzge-fyenyerezge mpaka ghose ghakanjila."

"Nanga uli Muwuso wakawa mwana wa phamphu pa nchito, mbwenu Soyaphi wali naye fyenyerezge/fyenyerezge-fyenyerezge kopa kuti kumachelo wangamupoka mpando."

Fyofyonthane[2]

This is from the verb "kufyofyonthana" to kiss each other.

'fyofyonthane' is in reference to a single act of kissing each other. If repeated, *'fyofyonthane-fyofyonthane'* is in reference to several acts of kissing each other.

"Ŵaliska ŵati ŵatuŵiska nthengwa, mbwenu Lazalo na Maria fyofyonthane/fyofy-onthane-fyofyonthane."

Fyofyonthe[2]

This comes from the verb "kufyofyontha" to kiss someone, or to draw liquid into one's mouth.

'fyofyonthe' is in reference to a single act of kissing, or sucking. If repeated, *'fyofyonhe-fyofyonthe'* is in reference to several acts of kissing someone (even if they do not respond), or several acts of sucking.

"Kulongola kiti wakumutemwa mwana wake, mbwenu mumatama mwake fyofyonthe/fyofyonthe-fyofyonthe."

"Kakumwa ako kakakhalapo, mbwenu Soyaphi fyofyonthe/fyofyonthe-fyofyonthe."

Fyogodo

This is derived from the verb "kufyogodola" to step on someone with intent to injure or hurt.

'fyogodo' is in reference to the actual contact resulting into injury or pain.

"Pakwamba ŵakaseŵelanga makola nkhanila, kweni paumalilo mbwenu Muwuso wali naye munyake fyogodo pa kalundi."

Fyonole

This is from the verb "kufyonola" to pull back the foreskin.

'fyonole' is in reference to the act of pulling back the foreskin.

"Soyaphi kuti walongole makola sing'anga chilonda icho wakaŵa nacho kunthazi, mbwenu nthazi yila fyonole."

Fyonthe[2]

This is from the verb "kufyontha" to sip.

'fyonthe' is in reference to the act of sipping. If repeated, *'fyonthe-fyonthe'* is in reference to continued acts of sipping and possibly even cleaning out the liquid.

"Wati wapika mphindi ya phele, mbwenu Dokiso phele lila dankha fyonthe."

"Chifukwa cha nyota, mbwenu Wanangwa tumaji uto tukaŵapo fyonthe-fyonthe."

Fyoo

This comes from the verb "kufyoteska" to create a narrow base.

'fyoo' is in reference to the narrowness at the end part of an object – as with a horn, or a garment. *'fyoo'* could also be used in reference, sarcastically, to narrow-mindedness.

"Takondwa wakutondeka kwenda makola chifukwa malaya ghachita kuti fyoo pa makongono."

"Nchindi nanga uli wakuchita nkhwesa, mahala pala wali ni fyoo."

Fyopo (also see "lizu")

This comes from the verb "kufyopola" to rip off skin.

'fyopo' is in reference to the ripping off of skin and exposing flesh.

"Khuni lamuwila pa msana Mayengiso mpaka msana wose fyopo."

Fyoropo(u)

This is from the verb "kufyoropola" to pull out an object from a confined space – as with a cork from a bottle.

'fyoropo(u)' is in reference to the popping out of the object being pulled.

"Tikaguza chigamu pa botolo mpaka fyoropo/fyoropu."

Fyozo

This comes from the verb "kufyozola" also to rip off, or tear away skin on impact and causing bleeding.

'*fyozo*' is in reference to that sudden loss of skin and the gush of blood.

"Chigomezgo wakawa mpaka khongono fyozo."

Fyule[2]

This comes from the verb "kufyula" to wipe – as in wiping tears, or dirt, or, in slang, to deny vehemently.

'*fyule*' is in reference to that act of wiping, or that act of complete denial to being involved. If repeated '*fyule-fyule*' is in reference to continued acts of wiping, or the act of a determined denial of involvement.

"Muwuso wati wageza mumawoko, mbwenu maji ghala fyule."

"Nanga uli ŵakayezga kumupanikizga, mbwenu Yezgaso makani ghose fyule/fyule-fyule."

Ga

'*ga*' is in reference to a situation where one cannot see through – as in heavy fog, dense smoke, heavy rain, or in darkness. Euphemistically, '*ga*' can also be used in reference to a situation where progress is at standstill because of hurdles.

"Mdima wachita kuti ga kuwalo."

"Nanga uli dazi ili nda chitatu kudumbilana, kweni nasono kuchali ga."

Gada[2]

This comes from the verb "kugadama" to lie on one's back, or to pull one's head back.

'gada' is in reference to that posture of lying on one's back, or leaning one's head backwards – voluntarily or having been knocked out. If repeated, *'gada-gada'* is in reference to more than one person, or animals lying on their backs or holding their heads backwards.

"Phyoka wakatimbika mpaka pasi gada."

"Tembani wakachita kuti mutu gada kuti wawone makola nyenyezi."

"Nkhalamu zafwasa – awonani zose zati gada-gada."

Gadabu[2]

This comes from the verbs "kugadabula" to turn over – as in cooking a stake, or as in turning a patient, or "kugadabuka" to rescind a position, or to roll over – as in a car overturning.

'gadabu' is in reference to that act of turning over or turning upside down. If repeated, *'gaabu-gadabu'* is in reference to several motions of turning upside-down, or rolling.

"Nkhuku yati yapha kulwande, mbwenu Zizipizgani nkhuku yila gadabu kuti yiphye yose."

"Galimoto yati yatheleleka pa musewu, mbwenu gadabu."

"Apo tose tikatenge tamuyowoya chinthu chimoza, mbwenu Lazalo gadabu tati tamba makani."

"Mumoyo mwati mwamuyamba, mbwenu Penjani gadabu-gadabu pa mphasa."

Gagawu

This comes from the verb "kugagawula" to forcibly rip off – as in removal of a bandage stuck to a wound.

'gagawu' is in reference to that act of forcefully peeling off the skin and exposing the raw inside.

"Apo tikawuskangapo bandeji pa chilonda, nachikumba wuwo mbwenu gagawu."

Galaganthi[2] or Ganthi[2]

These are from the verbs "kugalaganthila" and "kuganthila" to limp, or to walk with an uneven step.

'galaganthi' or *'ganthi'* is the act of limping. If repeated, *'galaganthi-galaganthi'* or *'ganthi-ganthi'* is in reference to several limps.

"Jando pakwenda wakuchita kuti galaganthi/ganthi chifukwa chakutupa khongono."

"Mbuzi yikachita kuti galaganthi-galaganthi/ganthi-ganthi pakwenda yati yapyoka kalundi."

Gamatu

This comes from the verb "kugamatula" to dig out a hard surface with large chunks of hard soil breaking off.

'gamatu' is in reference to the separation of mass as a result of digging – as in a piece of hard soil breaking off from the surface.

"Apo tikajimanga chiduli, dongo likachitanga kuti gamatu na kuwila mu nkhando."

Ganamphu

This comes from the verb "kuganamphula" to dislodge something – as with a tree from the ground, or a fingernail from a toe.

'ganamphu' is in reference to the sudden separation from main – as in a tree from the soil, or as in finger nail from a toe if in collision with a hard obstacle.

"Chigomezgo wakakhuŵala mpaka njoŵe ganamphu."

"Tikalimbana nacho chigodo mpaka ganamphu."

Ganthyaganthya

This is from the verb 'kuganthyama" to walk unsteadily because of being shoved or because of too much alchol.

'ganthyaganthya' is in reference to the act of walking unsteadily because of one's loss of balance – either through a sudden shove, a hard hit, or too much alcohol.

"Yatuta wati watimbika na nthonga mu mutu, mbwenu ganthyaganthya mpaka pasi kwii."

"Zizipizgani wakuchita kuti ganthyaganthya pakwenda chifukwa chakukhuta phele."

Ganu

This comes from the verb "kuganula" which is rather vulgar – to open one's thighs, or anus.

'ganu' is in reference to that act of opening one's inner side.

"Wati wagona chagada, mbwenu malundi ganu."

Gayawu

This is another vulgar word – coming from the verb "kugayawula" to open one's thighs widely.

'gayawu' is in reference to the opening up of one's thighs widely.

"Wati wavula dolozi, mbwenu nthangaloro gayawu."

Gege[2]

This is from the verb "kugega" to bypass, or skirt around, or to avoid.

'gege' is in reference to the act of bypassing, or avoiding. If repeated, *'gege-gege'* is in reference to total avoidance.

"Tiyezge mumalo mwakuti wajumphe pachikaya, mbwenu chikaya chila gege."

"Mumalo mwakuti Dunduzu walondole mudawuko wapakaya, iye mbwenu madoda ghose gege-gege nakukafika yekha kwa fumu."

Ghalaghala

'ghalaghala' is in reference to the act of climbing a tree – as with a lizard, or a motor vehicle climbing over a curb.

"Apo tikamuchimbizganga gunkhwe, iye mbwenu khuni ghalaghala."

"Galimoto yati yatondeka kukhweta, mbwenu muchiduli ghalaghala."

Go or Gote

These are from the verb "kugota" to end in a cul-de-sac.

'go' or 'gote' is the coming to an end of something – could be a process or an activity.

"Nanga uli Yesaya wakayezga kuchimbila ŵa, polisi paumalilo mbwenu go."

"Tati tafika pa libwe, mbwenu gote."

Godobu

This comes from the verb "kugodoboka" to cause to slide downwards, or, in slang, to die, or from the verb "kugodobola" to fell – as with a tree stump.

'godobu' is in reference to the motion of sliding downwards, or going down a slope, or turning upside down or, in slang, dying.

"Vula yati leke waka, mbwenu malibwe mu lupili nagho godobu."

"Uko tikusopa, mbwenu munyithu godobu."

"Khuni la muwanga tikalimbana nalo mpaka pa umalilo khuni lila godobu."

"Tati tajumpha Rukuru, mbwenu godobu mpaka mu Chiweta#."

Gombereske[2]

This is from the verb "kugombereska" to bend, or cause to form a curve.

'gombereske' is in reference to the act of bending an object, or forming a curve in an object. If repeated, *'gombereske-gombereske'* is in reference to the act of either making several curves in an object, or distorting it.

"Muwuso mumalo mwakuti wanyoloske mizele pa kulima, iye mbwenu gombereske/ gombereske-gombereske."

Gomoto(u) (also see "gumutu")

This is from the verb 'kugomotola" to break off a lump, or to separate a lump – as from hard ground, or a piece of cooked pumpkin from the shell.

'gomoto(u)' is in reference to the separation of mass in a lump form.

"Thanga likaŵa liweme – pakulya likatenge waka gomoto(u)."

Gompho

This comes from the verb "kugomphola" to doze.

'gompho' is in reference to the act of dozing or dozing off.

"Agogo sono apo ŵakhala nchito ni gompho."

Gong'o

This is from the verb "kugong'ola" to bang or to ram one's limb, such as an elbow, against a hard surface, or to bang someone with a stick.

'gong'o' is in reference to the bang or the hit against a hard surface.

"Nkatutuzgika mpaka mutu ku chimati gong'o."

"Kuti wamukalipiske munyake Soyaphi, mbwenu wali naye dala gong'o na chisulo."

Gongonyale[2]

This is from the verb "kugogonyala" to crimp or to be in curls.

'gongonyale' is the state of being creased or crimpled.

"Chifukwa cha kocha, mbwenu mahamba nagho gongonyale/gongonyale-gongonyale."

Gonthi[2] (see "ganthi")

This is from the verb "kugonthila" to limp.

'gonthi' is the act of a single limp. If repeated, *'gonthi-gonthi'* is in reference to continuous limping.

"Mabuchi wakuchita kuti gonthi/gonthi-gonthi pakwenda chifukwa cha kutupa kwa lundi."

Gonyo

This is from the verb "kugonyola" to cut off as when defecating or "kugonyoka" to be cut off – as with the last drop of dung.

'gonyo' is in reference to the falling off of the last piece – of dung or faeces.

"Wati wamala kujovwila, mbwenu paumalilo ka mchimba gonyo."

Gudubu[2]

This comes from the verbs "kugudubula" to overturn things, or "kugudubuka" to overturn.

'gudubu' is in reference to the motion of overturning. If repeated, *'gudubu-gudubu'* is in reference to continuous motions of rolling over.

"Apo Siyenji wakati wasonkhe moto, mbwenu mphika gudubu."

"Mabuleke ghati ghatondeka kukola, mbwenu galimoto yila gudubu."

Gulugutilu

This comes from the verb "kugulugutila" to sprint at high speed.

'gulugutilu' is in reference to the flash in speed – like "here and gone."

"Uko Lazalo wakupenja liswazu, mbwenu Soyaphi gulugutilu kwa ŵanyina.

Gumu

This comes from the verb "kugumula" to break a wall, or to pull down a building.

'gumu' is in reference to the breaking off of soil or lumps of wall.

"Wati waswa chiundo na musi, mbwenu chiundo chila gumu."

Gumutu

This comes from the verbs "kugumutula" to break in lumps or, "kugumutuka" to be broken in lumps.

'gumutu' refers to the actual falling off of mass – as from a wall, or as from a shell in case of a pumpkin.

"Thanga lati lapya, likachitanga kuti gumutu."

Gurumu

This comes from the verb "kugurumura" to scrub a body, or to clean a body by rubbing with something rough.

'gurumu' refers to that act of scrubbing, or cleaning off.

"Wati wamuthila maji mwana thupi lose, mbwenu Thokozani msana wa mwana wula gurunu na libwe."

Gutuzge[2]

This is from the verb "kugutuzga" to quickly cook or prepare a little sima.

'gutuzge' is in reference to a single fast turn of the cooking spoon as one prepares the sima. If repeated, *'gutuzge-gutuzge'* is in reference to the continuous fast process of preparing sima.

"Luwilo-luwilo, mbwenu Suzgika sima yake gutuzge/gutuzge-gutuzge kuti ŵalendo ŵalye."

Guu

'guu' is in reference to the wafting of bad odour across one's nostrils.

"Khuzwayo wakuchita kuti mowa guu apa wakhala."

Guyusuguyusu

This is from the verb "kuguyusuka" to have a coarse texture on the palate – as when eating a potato which is not done.

'guyusuguyusu' is in reference to the feel of lack of a smooth texture as one eats something that may be under-coocked.

"Mboholi zose zikuchita kuti guyusuguyusu pakulya chifukwa zindaphye."

Guze[2]

This is from the verb "kuguza" to pull.

'guze' is in reference to a single act of pulling. If repeated, *'guze-guze'* is in reference to several acts of pulling.

"Chandiwira wati wagona, mbwenu Mazaza bulangete lamunyake guze/guze-guze."

Gwagwalala

'gwagwalala' is in reference to stiffness in an object due to dryness – as in a dry leaf, or in a dried animal skin, or due to seizure – as if someone is attacked by an epileptic seizure. Euphemistically it can also be used in reference to the appearance of one whose health is waning or fading or drying up.

"Nchindi wakazilika mpaka thupi gwagwalala."

"Chifukwa cha chilala, ngoma zachita kuti gwagwalala muminda."

Gwamile[2]

This is from the verb "kugwamila" not to let go.

'gwamile' is in reference to the act of not wanting to share – or letting something free. If repeated, *'gwamile-gwamile'* is in reference to total closure of access to an object by others.

"Tapiwa wakayezga kumupempha yembe Zalelapi, kweni munyake uyu mbwenu yembe zose gwamile/gwamile-gwamile."

Gwede[2]

This comes from the verbs "kugwedela" to be wobbly, or shakey, or from the verb "kugwedezga" to shake.

'gwede' is in reference to a single wobble. If repeated *'gwede-gwede'* is in reference to complete looseness and therefore very wobbly - as with a loose joint.

"Jino usange lavunda, likwamba kuti gwede/gwede-gwede."

"Wati wawona kuti munyake wakugomphola, mbwenu wali naye gwede/gwede-gwede."

Gwedebu

This comes from the verb "kugwedebula" to unfold – as with a folded chair, or to dismantle or break loose – as with a latch on a door frame.

'gwedebu' is in reference to that sudden release or seperation of joints or hinges.

Temwa wati wafika, mbwenu Wongani mpando gwedebu kuti munyakhe wakhalepo."

"Lazalo wakalimbana nacho chijalo mpaka chijalo gwedebu."

Gwedu

This comes from the verb "kugwedula" to dismantle, or to cripple, or to maim.

'gwedu' is in reference to the falling apart of pieces once joined together, or to disabling – as in crippling one's knee.

"Uko Ndagha wakuguza thebulo, mbwenu lundi limoza gwedu."

"Zakeyo wakawa pasi kufuma mu khuni mpaka khongono gwedu."

Gweng'u or Gwenyu

These come from the verbs "kugweng'ula" or "kugwenyula" to hit or strike an object with a hard tool.

'gweng'u' or 'gwenyu' refer to that moment of impact and the thud.

"Uko ncheŵe yikuti yichimbire, Dokiso wali nayo gweng'u/gwenyu na nthonga."

Gwinyizge[2]

This comes from the verb "kugwinyizga" to tighten a noose or loop around an object (neck or leg).

'gwinyizge' or *'gwinyizge-gwinyizge'* is in reference to either a single act of fastening or several acts of tightening a noose to ensure security.

"Wati watola goda, mbwenu goda lila gwinyizge/gwinyizge-gwinyizge mu singo la mbuzi."

Halaghandu

This is from the verb "kuhalaghanduka" to get up.

'halaghandu' is in reference to the act of getting up from a sitting position, or from sleep, in readiness for action.

"Wati wapulika kuchemelezga, mbwenu Timeyo halaghandu apo wakakhala."

Hangayike[2]

This is from the verb "kuhangayika" to be confused, or to be at a loss, or to suffer at heart because of some serious event.

'hangayike' is in reference to that expression of confusion, loss, or fear of the unknown. If repeated, *'hangayike-hangayike'* is in reference to the feeling or appearance of total loss.

"Suzgika wati wapulika za yifwa yo ŵawiske, mbwenu mwana hangaike/hangaike-hangaike."

"Nyumba yati yaphya, Mzondi na muwoli wake mbwenu hangaike-hangayike."

Hehemu

This comes from the verb "kuhehemuka" to suddenly come to, or suddenly wake up because of a shock.

'hehemu' refers to that sudden awakening to reality.

"Uchizi wati wamuthila maji ghazizimu Tafwakose, mbwenu Tafwakose hehemu."

"Apo Lazalo wakatenge hehemu, nyumba yose yikawa kuti yakolela moto uheni!"

Hepu/hapu

This is derived from the verb "kuhepula" or "kuhapula" to sip.

'hepu' or *'hapu'* refers to the act of sipping a liquid.

"Wati wamupa bala, mbwenu mulwali yula bala lila dankha hepu/hapu."

Horohonyo

This is derived from the verb "kuhorohonya" to forcibly insert a stake into the anus.

'horohonyo' is in reference to the act of pushing a stake into the rear.

"Munkhungu yula wati wakoleka, mbwenu ŵathu ŵali naye horohonyo kunyuma na sungwi."

Horohoro

'*horohoro*' is in reference to exclaiming an intent to take advantage of a given situation – as with a rapist meeting a lonely female, or as with a thief coming across an exposed valuable.

"Wati wasanga mpukutu wa ndalama pa nthowa, Wezi wakachita kuti horohoro."

Hulukutu

'*hulukutu*' is in reference to a bad fall to the ground – as in a stampede, or from a bad stumble.

"Tawonga wati wamukolombezga Yezgani, mbwenu Yezgani mudongo hulukutu."

Hupu

This is from the verb "kuhupula" to drink in small mouthfuls.

'*hupu*' is in reference to the action of sipping, or taking a liquid in small mouthfuls.

"Chimwemwe wati wamala kulya, mbwenu msuzi wa nyama hupu."

Hwahwalala

'*hwahwalala*' is in reference to things being in abundance – as with fruits, livestock, or as in a bumper yield. '*hwahwalala*' however, could also be in reference to the act of falling to the ground in a heap – as in a knock-out, or it could be in reference to objects being in a disorderly state – as in an untidy room.

"Panyumba yakwithu, vyakulya ni hwahwalala."

"Soyaphi wakatimbika mpaka pasi hwahwalala."

"Alongosi ŵaleka vinthu hwahwalala mu nyumba."

Ilye[2]

This is from the verb "kulya" to eat, or to consume.

'*ilye*' is in reference to the act of eating. If repeated, '*ilye-ilye*' is in reference to the act of eating everything.

"Awonani mwana uyu – mbwenu dende pela ilye/ilye-ilye."

Imwe²

This is from the verb "kumwa" to drink.

'imwe' is in reference to the act of drinking. If repeated, *'imwe-imwe'* is in reference to the act of drinking it all.

"Wati watola maji, mbwenu imwe."

"Komani wati wanjila mu nyumba, mbwenu chindongwa icho chikakhalapo imwe-imwe."

Jagada

This comes from the verb "kujagadala" to be out of line and not fitting together – as with teeth.

'jagada' is in reference to something like teeth not fitting together with some jutting out. *'jagada'* could also be in reference to a sudden sour twist in events.

"Tumbikani mino ghake ghakuchita kuti jagada mu mulomo."

"Apo tikatenge milandu yamala makola, muhanya uno mbwenu vinthu jagada chifukwa cha umboni upya."

Jang'anda

This comes from the verb "kujang'andala" also to be out of control, or out of order.

'jang'anda' is in reference to a situation that has lost control or order, or has suddenly come to a stalemate.

"Chifukwa chakufika kwa Chiphwafu, mbwenu vinthu jang'anda pa mphala."

Jegedu

This comes from the verb "kujegedula" to break one's skin using a finger nail.

'jegedu' is in reference to the action of breaking skin through use of finger nail.

"Apo ŵakaseŵelanga, mwenu Thokozani wali naye Tamala jegedu pa kawoko na njoŵe."

Jejenthu

This is from the verb "kujejenthula" also to bite off a piece – as when eating an apple.

'jejenthu' is the act of slicing off a piece using one's teeth.

"Fumbamtima wati wapawula yembe yambula kukhwima yila, mbwenu wali nayo jejenthu."

Jemphu

This comes from the verb "kujemphula" to bite off a piece – as with a fruit.

'jemphu' is in reference to the act of biting-off.

"Pambele wandasuke yembe, mbwenu Masozi yembe yila jemphu."

Jemu

This comes from the verb "kujemula" also to bite off a piece – as when eating sima or a piece of meat.

'jemu' is the act of biting off.

"Pambele Chiukepo wandabwite pa msuzi, mbwenu thozi lila jemu."

Jeng'enthu (see "jegedu")

This comes from the verb "kujeng'enthula" to cut skin and and expose tissue using a sharp object – could be a finger-nail or a tooth.

'jeng'enthu' is in reference to that act of a sudden savage bite or cut into skin.

"Soyaphi wali naye munyake jeng'enthu pa msana mpaka ndopa ntho."

"Uko wakonkha, mbwenu bele laŵanyina jeng'enthu."

Jenthu

This is from the verb "kujenthula" also to bite off a piece.

'jenthu' is the act of biting off.

"Wati wapika waka yembe, mbwenu wali nayo jenthu."

Jigida[2]

'jigida' is in reference to a woman's breast standing firm. If repeated, 'jigidajigida' is in reference to the up-and-down movements of breasts – as with a woman walking briskly.

"Nozgechi pala wimilila, mabele ghakuchita kuti jigida."

"Tamandenji pala wakwenda, mabele ghakuchita kuti jigidajigida."

Jike²

This is from the verb "kujika" to dig one's heels into the soil and remain firm.

'jike' is in reference to the act of remaining rooted and firm. If repeated, 'jike-jike' is in reference to total determination not to be shaken.

"Apo Tembani wakati waguguze mbuzi, mbwenu mbuzi yila jike."

"Apo ŵasiliksli na ŵapolisi ŵakaguzananga na chingwe, mwenu ŵose jike-jike."

Jikhe²

This is from the verb "kujikha" to disembark.

'jikhe' is in reference to the act of disembarking. If repeated, 'jikhe-jikhe' is in reference (usually) to acts of disembarking by more than one person.

"Ndati ndafika, mbwenu galimoto yila jikhe."

"Tati tafika, mbwenu galimoto yila jikhe-jikhe."

Jinthe²

This comes from the verb "kujintha" to drive a stake into the ground.

'jinthe' is in reference to the act of driving a single stake into the ground. If repeated, 'jinthe-jinthe' is in reference to the act of planting or driving several stakes into the ground.

"Mazaza wati watola mkondo, mbwenu pasi jinthe."

"Dumisani dimba lake wachita kuti makuni jinthe-jinthe mulwandi mose kopa kuti ng'ombe zingamulyela."

Jiti

This is from the verb "kujitika" to climb down.

'jiti' is the act of climbing down.

"Galimoto yati yimilila, mbwenu Wezi jiti."

Joko

This comes from the verb "kujokola" to poke sharply, or to goad.

'joko' is the act of poking, or of goading to provoke action.

"Njoka yati yanjila ku khululu, mbwenu Soyaphi wali nayo joko na swato."

Joo

'*joo*' is in reference to the act of standing still – as with a soldier on guard.

"Awonani ka kalulu kimilila joo."

Jowo

This comes from the verb "kujowola" to leave behind, or to dump.

'*jowo*' is in reference to the act of leaving something behind, or the act of dumping.

"Fulatela wakamuleka munyake jowo ku thengele."

"Soyaphi wakati tole waka mbwenu mwanakazi jowo pa kaya."

Ju-ju²

This is also from the verb "kujuta" to struggle for freedom once tied up around the legs.

'*ju-ju*' is in reference to a single stroke of struggling. If repeated, '*ju-ju-ju-ju*' is in reference to prolonged strokes of struggling whether when tied up, or in a tussle or even in speech.

"Soyaphi ŵati ŵamukaka malundi, mbwenu wambapo ju-ju/juju-juju kuti panji wangasutula vingwe."

"Madoda ghati ghamupa mwaŵi kuti naye wayowoyepo, mbwenu Lazalo ju-ju pakuyowoya."

Julire²

This is from the verb "kujulira" to open up – as in opening a small enclosure to let domestic animals out, or to allow access – as in someone opening a door for one to enter.

'*julire*' is in reference to the act of opening for exiting. If repeated, '*julire-julire*' is in reference specifically to opening access in several parts of an enclosure for domestic animals to have unrestricted access out.

"Namulenjilenji, mbwenu Nthembozawo nkhuku zake julire."

"Pakati pa usiku, mbwenu Soyaphi ng'ombe julire-julire."

Julizge²

This is from the verb "kujulizga" either (i) to awaken someone at their home at an odd hour or (ii) to forcibly enter someone's home at night.

'julizge' is in reference to the act of causing one to open up. If repeated, *'julizge-julizge'* is in reference to the act of awakening several households

"Pakati pa usiku, mbwenu Lazalo NyaPhiri julizge."

"Uthenga wa yifwa wati wafika, mbwenu ŵazukulu nyumba zose julizge-julizge."

Junchwa

'junchwa' is in reference to the act of being lonely after being dumped or deserted.

"Chifukwa cha pa mulomo pake, ŵanyake ŵakamuleka Mafunase junchwa pa yifwa ya mkulu wake."

Jungululu/Jungununu

This comes from the verb "kujunguluka" or "kujungunuka" to suddenly feel warm in the tummy – as when in panic, or afraid, or in need of a toilet.

'jungululu' or *'jungununu'* is in reference to the movement in bowels as when one needs to run to a toilet because of some scare.

"Cheruzgo wati wamanya kuti wakoleka, mbwenu mumoyo jungululu/jungununu."

Junyunthu

This comes from the verb "kujunyunthula" to cause to bounce, or "kujunyunthuka" to bounce off against hard ground, or against a wall.

'junyunthu' refers to the bounce, or bouncing off without being harmed.

"Tayala lati lapozomoka pa chanya pa galimoto, mbwenu pasi junyunthu."

Juti²

This is from the verb "kujuta" to fight off – as with a cow fighting not to have its hind legs tied or restricted.

'juti' is in reference to that single strained movement because legs are tied together. If repeated, *'juti-juti'* refers to repeated strained movements as in an animal trying to move normally but cannot because its feet are restrained.

"Chifukwa ng'ombe yikakakika malundi ghakumanyuma, mbwenu pakwenda juti/juti-juti."

Juu

'juu' is in reference to the warming up of a tummy as a result of either taking something warm, or hard liquor or because of eating something poisonous.

"Namunyinu manyi ndalyachi – mumoyo mukuchita kuti juu."

Jwa

'jwa' is in reference to the act of jumping and plunging into a deep hole, or deep waters, or deep trouble.

"Chakufwa wakachimbila mpaka mu dambo jwa."

Phyoka wati wahala mwanakazi yula, mbwenu mu visuzgo jwa."

Jwadi

This is from the verb "kujwadika" to place into – as placing an object at the bottom of a container.

'jwadi' is in reference to getting into deep space.

"Chifukwa cha kwenda maso ghali mu chnya, Nezala wakazakachulukila mu mbuna jwadi."

Jwadike

Also from the verb "kujwadika" to leave, or place something in some place with intent to hide.

'jwadike' is in reference to the act of dipositing something in some hidden place.

"Towela wati wawona kuti kukwiza Mafunase, mbwenu nyama yake mu mbiza jwadike."

Jwanthi

This comes from the verb "kujwantha" or "kujwanthila" to jump over, or to omit, or to skip.

'jwanthi' is thus in reference to the act of jumping over, or skipping.

"Khuni lati lawa na kujala nthowa, mbwenu Chananga khuni lila jwanthi kuti walutilile na ulendo wake."

"Apo Thapisoni wakafikanga pafupi kuti naye wapokeleko ngoma, mbweu ŵali naye jwanthi."

Kaku

This is from the verb "kukakuka" to rise slowly but steadily — as in someone who has been ill for a long period, or as in weeds spreading.

'*kaku*' is in reference to the slow but steady rise of one who has been in one position for long, or as in a burst of weeds in a once clean patch.

"Zovu yati yachiluskika apo yikagona, mbwenu zovu yila kaku."

"Mu munda wakwithu utheka wachita kuti kaku."

Kamu[2]

This comes from the verb "kukamuka" to dry up.

'*kamu*' is in reference to the drying up of water or moisture — as in a well, mouth, or river bed. '*kamu*' can also be used in reference to the coming of an end to having resources. If repeated, '*kamu-kamu*' is in reference to total lack of fluid or moisture in a given place.

"Chilala chati chafika, mbwenu maji nagho kamu mu dambo."

"Wati watola mwanakazi wachitatu Yatuta, nakalinga mbwenu chuma chose kamu."

"Lumbani wati wakoleka, mbwenu mu mulomo mata kamu-kamu."

Kang'alala

'*kang'alala*' is in reference to the act of falling backwards as from a vicious push or as in someone who has fainted.

"Mzondi ŵakamulikita mpaka pasi kang'alala."

Kanganu or Kangazu

This comes from the verbs "kukanganula" or "kukangazula" to forcefully separate two objects stuck together as with metal, or legs.

'*kanganu*' or "*kangazu*' is in reference to the act of separating two objects or the act of opening up legs.

"Tati tatimba vijalo vya galimoto na nyondo, mbwenu vijalo vila kanganu."

"Wati wagona cha gada, mbwenu malundi kanganu/kangazu kuti ŵa sing'anga ŵawone suzgo lake."

Kankhamu

This comes from the verb "kukankhamuka" to come out of a comma or serious illness. Euphestically, the verb "kukankhamuka" can be used to mean coming out of deep poverty.

'kankhamu' is in reference to the act of awakening from an abyss into normality once again.

"Ŵati ŵamumweska bala Lazalo, mbwenu pa mphasa kankhamu."

"Malonda ghati ghakola, mbwenu a Yezgaso nayo kankhamu."

Kanu

This comes from the verb "kukanula" also to separate two objects stuck together, or to open one's thighs.

'kanu' refers to the coming off of separation between two objects stuck together, or the opening of thighs.

"Tikalimbana navyo visulo mpaka pa umalilo kanu."

"Wati wamuwiska pasi, mbwenu malundi ghala kanu."

Kata-kata

This is from the verb "kukatakata" to shiver – as from cold or fear.

'kata-kata' is the act of shivering or trembling.

"Mayengiso wakuchita kuti kata-kata chifukwa cha wofi."

Kazule[2]

This is from the verb "kukazula" to poison one's palate because of eating something unacceptable. Euphemistically, "kukazula" can mean to disturb one's normal good health.

'kazule' is in reference to the fouling of one's palate or self. If repeated, *'kazulekazule'* is in reference to a complete fouling of one's taste or self.

"Wati walya chule, mbwenu Chananga mu mulomo kazule/kazulekazule."

"Wati wanjila ku chokolo kula, mbwenu Soyaphi kazule/kazulekazule."

Kazuzge[2]

This is from the verb "kukazuzga" to cause evil effects on someone – could be through poison, or some unacceptable input – language or behaviour.

'kazuzge' is in reference to the act of injecting something unacceptable into someone. If repeated, *'kazuzge-kazuzge'* is in reference to total soiling.

"Wati wamala kuphika dende, mbwenu dende lila kazuzge kuti wapweteke musweni wake."

"Nanga uli Chimango wakamanyanga kuti iye ni mulwali, mbwenu dala muwoli wake kazuzge/kazuzge-kazuzge."

"Mumalo mwakuti mwana ŵamusamizge nkhalo yiweme, mbwenu mwana kazuzge-kazuzge mwakuti sonoo walije na nchindi yili yose."

Khabu

This is from the verb "kukhabula" to cause fluid to suddenly splash, or the verbs "kukhabuka" to splash, or "kukhabuska" to cause to splash, or to cause a heart miss a beat because of some alarm.

'khabu' refers either to the sudden splash of fluid in a container, or the sudden heart beat as a result of some disturbance.

"Apo Siyenji wakathwikanga chipindi pa mutu, mbwenu maji ghala khabu."

"Ulanda wati wapulika za yifwa, mbwenu mtima khabu."

Khapi

This comes from the verb "kukhapila" to choke, or to drink in gulps, or the verb "kukhapizga" to cause one to choke.

'khapi' is in reference to the act of gasping as one struggles to breathe, or struggles in taking something in bulk.

"Ŵati ŵamukhinya ku singo Chigomezgo, mbwenu mwana yula khapi."

"Sunganani wati wawa mu dambo, mbwenu maji khapi."

"Mwana pakumuchinga bala, wakachitanga kuti khapi."

Khazge[2]

This is from the verb "kukhazga" to waylay, or to block, or to wait in expectation.

'khazge' is in reference to the act of waylaying, or the act of waiting in anticipation. If repeated *'khazge-khazge'* is in referenmce to an act of total blockade.

"Soyaphi wati wamanya kuti Uchizi wakwiza kufuma ku dambo, mbwenu panthowa khazge."

"Uko Zizipizgani wakujima mbeŵa, mbwenu Lazalo makululu ghose khazge-khazge."

Khechule[2]

This is from the verb "kukhechula" to tear apart, or to tear apart someone's views, opinion, or proposal.

'khechule' is in reference to a single tear. If repeated, *'khechule-khechule'* is in reference to total destruction through tearing, or a continued vicious attack on someone's views to the point of rendering those views useless.

"Maria wati wamala kuŵazga kalata, mbwenu kalata yila khechule/khechule-khechule" kuwopa kuti a sambizgi ŵangamukola nayo."

"Wati wafika Mathangeni pa mphala, mbwenu umboni wose uwo ukapelekeka, khechule-khechule."

Khee

This derives from the verb "kukheska" to enter into an enclosure, or to exit an enclosure without decorum or permission.

'khee' is in reference to the sudden entry or exit – as into a thicket, or through a kraal, or out of some other enclosure.

"Nausiku pakati, mbwenu Chawezi munyumba yamunyake khee."

"Kuti waleke kukoleka, mbwenu Masida pa thengele khee."

Khi

This comes from the verb "kukhinya" to strangle.

'khi' refers to that act of strangling.

"Masozi wali naye munyake pa songo khi."

Kho[3]

This is from the verb "kukhoma" to knock in – as with a hammer.

'kho' is in reference to a single knock. If repeated, *'kho-kho-kho'* is in reference to several knocks, but could also be in reference to acts of killing – as in killing a snake.

"Kuti wamuyambe munyake, mbwenu pa mutu kho."

"Mumalo mwakuti ŵamuleke munkhungu yula, ŵanthu munthu yula mpaka kho-kho-kho."

Khojole[2]

This is from the verb "kukhojola" to manually remove shrubs, or small branches from a tree with little care.

'khojole' is in reference to a single act of manually cutting off a shrub or a small branch from the main tree. If repeated, *'khojole-khojole'* is in reference to several efforts of pulling away shrubs covering a wide area.

"Pambele Lazalo wandambe kulima, mbwenu vivwati yose khojole/khojole-khojole."

Khong'oske[2]

This is from the verb "kukhong'oska" to knock – as on a door

'khong'oske' is in reference to a single act of knocking. If, repeated, *'khong'oske-khong'oske'* is in reference to acts of several knocks.

"Wati wafika pa chijalo Zizwani, mbwenu khong'oske kuti ŵamjulileko."

"Wati wafika pa chikaya mu usiku, mbwenu nyumba zose khong'oske-khong'oske, kweni nayumo wakamujulilako."

Khonyo

This comes from the verb "kukhonyola" to break off a piece from the main without due care – as with a piece of wood from a log.

'khonyo' is in reference to the falling off of the piece.

"Pala ukuwona ka mchimba khonyo, ndiko kuti kujovwila wamala."

Khowo or Khowole[2]

This comes from the verb "kukhowola" to knock someone along joints, usually with something hard, or, on the other extreme, to dislocate.

'khowo' or *'khowole'* refers to a single act of knocking someone with a hard object or a single act of dislocating. If repeated, *'khowole-khowole'* is in reference to several acts of knocking or dislocating.

"Zikani uko wakuchita chiwawa mu kalasi, wakachulukila pa mutu khowo."

"Soyaphi wati wamalizgika, mbwenu makongono khowole/khowole-khowole."

Khoyowu(o)

This comes from the verb "kukhoyowola" to break off a cob of maize from the stalk.

'khoyowu' refers to dislodging of the cob from the stalk.

"Lazalo wati wanjila mu munda, mbwenu chingoma khoyowu(o)."

Khubazge²

This comes from the verb "kukhubazga" to mess up someone, or to cause someone to err.

'khubazge' is in reference to the act of inducing an error. If repeated, *'khubazge-khubazge'* is in reference to continuous acts of messing up someone.

"Apo kuti kwakhala nyengo yichoko kumalizga masambilo, mbwenu Lazalo Tiwonge yula khubazge/khubazge/khubazge."

Khufu

This comes from the verb "kukhufula" to kick into something using a foot or hand in case of a container, usually out of disgust, and, at times, also causing a spill.

'khufu' is the act of kicking something and sometimes also spilling out contents.

"Uko Tembani wakuti wachimbile, Masida wali naye khufu mumatako."

"Chifukwa chakukwiya, mbwenu Mzondi wali nacho chihengo cha ufu khufu."

Khufule²

Also from the verb "kukhufula" to strike an object with the foot or palm with the intent to throw out contents.

'khufule' is in reference to the single act of a rough kick or shove of a container of sort. If repeated, *'khufule-khufule'* is in reference to several kicks, or shoves of objects containing something and causing spills.

"Ndagha chihengo cha ufu chila mbwenu dala khufule."

"Manyi nchifukwa chakuti wakaloŵela, mbwenu vihengo vya ufu vila khufule-khufule."

Khule²

This is from the verb "kukhula" to remove – as in tooth extraction, or as with an axe from its handle, or as with a tyre from the hub.

'khule' is in reference to the act of extracting, or dismantling. If repeated, *'khule-khule'* refers to repeated acts of extraction or dismantling.

"Mhaŵi wati wamala kutema makuni ghake, mbwenu mbavi khule."

"Mino gha agogo ghati ghavunda, mbwenu mino ghose ghala khule-khule."

Khulule²

This is from the verb "kukhulula" to pull out yarn or thread from a piece of cloth or from something woven.

'khulule' is in reference to the act of pulling out a thread. If repeated, *'khulule-khulule'* is in reference to removal of all yarn.

"Fidesi wati wawona kuti wanangiska kasonelo, mbwenu wuzu wula khulule."

"Ŵanyina ŵati ŵamala kuluka swetala, mbwenu Tawina wali nayo khulule-khulule."

Khuma²

This comes from the verb "kukhumata" to sit in dejection with hands folded across the chest.

'khuma' refers to that posture of loneliness and dejection – as in a person folding their shoulders or hands at the loss of a loved one, or because of cold. If repeated *'khuma-khuma'* is in reference to either repeated behaviour of dejection or in reference to a crowd seating or walking in dejection.

"Awonani Nyembezi wachita kuti khuma pa khonde chifukwa cha mphepo."

"Apo tikafikanga pa yifwa, tikasanga ŵanthu ŵali khuma/khuma-khuma."

Khutu²

This is from the verbs "kukhutula" to offload, or "kukhutuska," also to offload, or "kukhutuka" to be off-loaded.

'khutu' is in reference to the dropping of some mass of something. If repeated, *'khutu-khutu'* is in reference to a continuous drop of heavy mass.

"Apo galimoto yikawanga, mbwenu katundu yose khutu."

"Ŵati ŵatumbula chitufya, mafila ghakachita kuti khutu-khutu."

Khutuze²

This is from the verb "kukhutuza" to rip off, or to impoverish, or to let down.

'khutuze' is in reference to a single act of ripping off, or letting down. If repeated, *'khutuze-khutuze'* is in reference to ripping off someone to the extent of making one a pauper.

"Lazalo wati wasonga Mzamose, nakalinga musungwana wali naye khutuze/khutuze-khutuze mwakuti sono Lazalo wakulenga chitima."

Khwa

'khwa' is in reference to the act of landing on the ground – as with a bird, or a plane – or, at times, also applied in reference to the landing of a human as a result of a fall.

"Uku tikulaŵiska muchanya, mbwenu kayuni kala pasi khwa."

"Khuzwayo ŵakamulikita mpaka pasi khwa."

Khwachapu or Khwachapule²

These are from the verb "kukhwachapula" to tick off, or to mark with a tick.

'khwachapu' or *'khwachapule'* is the act of ticking off. If repeated, *'khwachapule-khwachapule'* is in reference to ticking off more than once.

"Asambizi ŵati ŵawona kuti ndalemba makola, mbwenu pa pepala pala khwachapu."

"Asambizi ŵati ŵawona kuti ziŵalo zose natola, mbwenu khwachapule-khwachapule."

Khwache²

This is from the verb "kukhwacha" to put a line through a page or paragraph, denoting cancellation.

'khwache' is the act of putting a line through a page or a paragraph. If repeated, 'khwache-khwache' is in reference to putting several lines through a page or part of it as cancelation.

"Ndati ndawona kuti zgolo nindalembe makola, mbwenu zgolo lila khwache."

"Asambizi ŵati ŵawona kuti vyose ivyo nkhalemba vikaŵa vyauzeleza, mbwenu vyose khwache-khwache."

Khwe

This comes from the verb "kukhweta" to make a sharp turn.

'khwe' refers to the act of suddenly changing direction.

"Kuti tili pafupi kufika pa Boma, mbwenu galimoto yila khwe kulazga ku Thoza."

"Mumalo mwakuti wazgole mu wunenesko, iye mbwenu khwe.

Khwefule[2]

This is from the verb "kukhwefula" either to reduce to size – as with the waste band of a pair of trousers, or euphemistically to floor someone.

'khwefule' is in reference to either a single act of reducing size, or one act of shoving off someone. If repeated, 'khwefule-khwefule' is in reference to continuous acts of down-sizing, or several acts of flooring people.

"Pakuti buluku likaŵa likulu mu chiwuno kwa ine, mbwenu a telala ŵali nalo khwefule/khwefule-khwefule kuti niyane nalo."

"Matata Sokayawo nga wali nankhongono – ŵanthu ŵali naye khwefule-khwefule."

Khwelele

This is from the verb "kukhwelelesa" to cause an axe blade to be disloged from the axe-handle.

'khwelele' is in reference to the dislodgement of an axe handle.

"Apo Masida wakakwelanga mukhuni na mbavi pa phewa, mbwenu mbavi yila khwelele."

Khwengenu[2]

This comes from the verb "kukhwengwena" to scrape one's buttocks or anus against the ground.

'khwengwenu' refers to the act of rubbing buttocks against the ground or soil. If repeated, *'khwengwenu-khwengwenu'* is in reference either to repeated acts of scraping against the ground, or it is in reference to subservient behaviour.

"Mumalo mwakuti Khoti wajipipe makola, mbwenu pasi khwengwenu."

"Awonani Mdaghanjala wakuchita kuti khwengwenu/khwengwenu-khwengwenu kwa a fumu chifukwa cha wofi/nchindi."

Khwetu

This is derived from the verbs "kukhwetula" to dislodge from a holder – as with a spear from its handle, or "kukwetuka" to be dislodged from a handle, or as with an axe blade from an axe handle.

'khwetu' refers to the actual dislodgement or separation of the spear/arrow from the handle.

"Uko wakuti waponye mukondo, mbwenu mkondo ula khwetu."

Khweze²

This is from the verb "kukhweza" to clear household objects in a particular area of the house – as with kitchenware in the kitchen, or objects in the bedroom so that the room looks tidied up.

'khweze' is in reference to a single act of tiding-up. If repeated, *'khweze-khweze'* is in reference to a done deal: all tiding-up done.

"Tati tamala kulya, mbwenu Tasokwa mbale zila khweze."

"Kuchali kundafipe, mbwenu Tiwonge munyumba mula khweze-khweze."

Khwii

'khwii' is is in reference to a condition of withdrawal – as in someone who does not want to participate in anything, or as with someone not cheerful. *'khwi'* can also be used in reference to poor or unpleasant weather.

"Tiyezge apo wakhala ni khwii nyengo yose."

Muhanya uno kundache makola – kuwalo kwachita kuti khwii."

Khwinya² or Khwinyu

These come from the verbs "kukhwinyata" to shrink, or to recoil, or to fold one's legs, or "kukhwinyula" to tighten one's anus.

'khwinya' is in reference to the act of recoiling, or shrinking, or being subdued. If repeated, *'khwinya-khwinya'* is in reference to a state of hopelessness – as in plants that are wilting, or being in a state of subjugation – as to a state where people are walking about in fear of the unknown.

"Mphepo yati yamupweteka, mbwenu Chawezi khwinya pa kugona."

"Nezala umo wali kuwelako ku ukaidi, apo wakhala ni khwinya-khwinya sono."

'khwinyu' however, is in reference to the short closing movements of the anus.

"Chiskuli chati chamukola, mbwenu Lazalo muchaza khwinyu."

Khwinyirizge²

This is derived from the verb "kukhwinyirizga" to persevere under the pressure of discomfort or pain.

'khwinyirizge' is in reference to the single effort of perseverance. If repeated, *'khwinyirizge-khwinyirizge'* is in reference to one's sustained determination not to succumb to pressure.

"Ku thondo kwati kwamukola Chiukepo, mbwenu khwinyirizge kopa mzinda wa womama."

"Nanga uli mumoyo mukajulika, mwana yula mbwenu khwinyirizge-khwinyirizge."

Khwizu²

This comes from the verb "kukhwizuka" to feel indignant, or to recoil inwards because of disappointment, or frustration, or in anger.

'khwizu' is in reference to the act, or facial expression of withdrawal as a result of disappointment. If repeated, *'khwizu-khwizu'* is in reference to serious self withdrawal.

"Muwuso wakuchita kuti khwizu/khwizu-khwizu madazi ghano chifukwa cha kufelula visola."

Kokomu²

This stems from the verb "kukokomoka" to roar, or to make a loud hoarse sound, or to shout in anger.

'kokomu' is in reference to the action of "roaring" or "shouting."

"Uphalazgi wati wamba, ŵaliska mbwenu kokomu."

"Pambele wandatayike, wakachita kuti kokomu-kokomu."

Kokoto

This comes from the verb "kukokotola" to look alike, or to resemble.

'kokoto' is in reference to total resemblance – as with a child looking very similar to a parent, or as with identical twins, or with a child to any other member of the family.

"Chigomezgo watola a gogo ŵake kokoto."

Kolele²

This is from the verb "kukolela" to hold.

'kolele' is in reference to the act of holding. If repeated, 'kolele-kolele' is in reference to the act of holding more than one thing.

"Phyoka wati wapokela nthuli ya nyama, mbwenu mukawoko kolele."

"Lazalo na Soyaphi ŵati ŵapokela nthuli zawo za nyama, mbwenu mumawoko ghawo kolele-kolele."

Kolokoto²

This comes from the verb "kukolokota" to scrape, or clean with something sharp. In slang, the verb can also mean to irk.

'kolokoto' is in reference to a single stroke of a scrape against a surface – as on something metalic, or the surface of a body so as to provoke. If repeated, 'kolokoto-kolokoto' refers to the continuous acts of scraping.

"Kuti wawuskemo vigongota mbwenu Malizgani sefuliya yila kolokoto/kolokoto-kolokoto na sipuni."

"Kuti wamukalipiske munyake, mbwenu wali naye pa mutu kolokoto."

Kolole²

This is from the verb "kukolola" to harvest.

'kolole' is in reference to a single act of harvesting. If repeated, 'kolole-kolole' is in reference to the act of completing the harvest.

"Ngoma zati zamila, mbwenu Phelile ngoma zila kolole/kolole-kolole."

Kolombezge²

This is from the verb "kukolombezga" to entwine, or to wedge between legs so as to floor somebody.

'kolombezge' is the act of entwining or wedging. If repeated, *'kolombezge-kolombezge'* is in reference to the act of total entwining of an object.

"Uko Komani wakuti wachimbile, mbwenu Khuzwayo wali naye kolombezge mu malundi."

"Mtaŵa wachita kuti kolombezge-kolombezge khuni lose."

Kombe²/kombelezge²

This is from the verbs "kukomba" to scoop something edible from a plate using one's forefinger, or "kukombelezga" to clean off the last particles of food from a plate using one's forefinger or tongue.

'kombe' or *'kombelezge'* is in reference to a single scoop from the plate. If repeated, *'kombe-kombe'* or *'kombelezge-kombelezge'*, is in reference to repeated swipes resulting in leaving the plate virtually clean.

"Wati wamala bala mu mbale, mbwenu Chimwemwe mbale yila kombe/kombe-kombe."

"Wati wamalizga kulya sima, mbwenu Lazalo mbale ya msuzi kombelezge/kombelezge-kombelezge."

Komo (also see "fyopo")

This comes from the verb "kukomola" to strip off bark, or skin.

'komo' is in reference to the sudden strip of bark or skin and the exposure of stem or flesh.

"Mthakati yikamuganda njinga mpaka lundi komo."

Komo or Komoke

These come from the verbs "kukomola" to cause one to lose consciousness, or "kukomoka" to faint.

'komo' is in reference to the act of losing consciousness.

"Uko ŵakuchimbila naye ku chipatala, mbwenu mwana yula komo pa nthowa.

'komoke' is also in reference to the act of fainting.

"Uko ŵakumugwaza nyeleti, mbwenu mwana yula komoke."

Kong'onthe[2]

This is from the verb "kukong'ontha" to knock, or to knock down, or to rap a hard surface.

'kong'onthe' is in reference to a single rap on a surface, or a beating. If repeated, "kongonthe-kong'onthe" is in reference to several acts of striking.

"Nyengo yati yakwana, mbwenu Lazalo belo kong'onthe."

"Chifukwa cha uzaghali, Sinya ŵanthu ŵali naye kong'onthe-kong'onthe."

Konkhoske[2]

This is from the verb "kukonkhoska" to explain in detail.

'konkhoske' is in reference to the act of explaining in full. If repeated, 'konkhoske-konkhoske' is in reference to the act of not leaving out any detail.

"Wumba wati wazomelezga kuti Yatuta naye wayowoyepo, mbwenu Yatuta maghanoghano ghake ghose konkhoske/konkhoske-konkhoske."

Konye

This is derived from the verb "kukonya" to crease – as with a piece of paper, or to crush with palms – as with a morsel.

'konye' is in reference to the single act of creasing, or crushing using one's palms. If repeated, 'konye-konye' is in reference to repeated creasing or crushing using palms.

"Wati wamenya sima, mbwenu sima yila konye."

"Yonamu wati wamanya kuti kalata njilwani, mbwenu kalata yila konye-konye nakutaya mu chimbuzi."

Konyombu

This comes from the verb "kukonyombola" to dislodge – as with a maize cob from the stem.

'konyombu' is in reference to that act of dislodging the cob.

"Munkhwele njile waka mu munda, mbwenu ngoma konyombu."

Koromu²

This comes from the verb "kukoromora" to roar – as with a lion, or to cough hoarsely.

'koromu' refers to that hoarse and throaty roar, or the sound of a hoarse cough. If repeated, *'koromu-koromu'* is in reference to repeated hoarse throaty sounds.

"Apo wakhala Timoti wakuchita kuti koromu pa kuhosomola.

"Nkharamu zikuchita kuti koromu-koromu ku Chimaliro."

Kudyu²/Kulukudyu²

This comes from the verb "kukudyula" to gulp, or drink hastily - as with fluids. If repeated, *'kudyu-kudyu/kulukudyu-kulukudyu'* refers to repeated fast gulps of fluid.

'kudyu' or *'kulukudyu'* refers to that quick gulping down the throat.

"Wati wamwa maji, mbwenu kudyu/kulukudyu."

"Mwana ŵati bamukola ku mphuno, mbwenu bala lila kudyu-kudyu/kulukudyu-kulukudyu."

Kukute²

This is from the verb "kukukuta" to gnaw, or to chew to the bone.

'kukute' is in reference to gnawing and cracking a bone in readiness to swallow the fragments. If repeated, *'kukute-kukute'* is in reference to thorough cracking of a bone – as with a dog cracking a bone.

"Mdaghanjala wati wamalizga kulya mulezi wa nkhuku, mbwenu chiwanga chila kukute/kukute-kukute."

Kuli-kuli

This is from the verb "kukulika" to be bare, or without the natural or usual covering – as with a playing field that has lost its grass.

'kuli-kuli' is in reference to total lack of cover of grass.

"Pawalo pa nyumba yakwithu pali kuli-kuli."

"Mu Chikangawa madazi ghano mwachita kuti kuli-kuli."

Kulumu

This is from the verb "kukulumuka" to slip through a surface, or to be slippery '*kulumu*' refers to the slipping of an object over a surface or through one's hold because the object is slimy – as with a wet bar of soap.

"Nanga vula yingawa uli-we pa nyumba ya malata, maji ni kulumu."

"Nyengo yose wakayezganga kukola somba na mawoko, mbwenu somba kulumu."

Kulunthu[2]

This derives from the verb "kukulunthuka" to squirm, or to wriggle.

'*kulunthu*' is in reference to that single twitch. If repeated, '*kulumthu-kulunthu*' is in reference to those continous wriggles (also see '*ziliku- ziliku*').

"Mwana wati wawa pasi, mbwenu tasanga mwana kurunthu."

"Pakufwa Lazalo wakachita kuti kulunthu-kulunthu."

Kulure[2]

This is from the verb "kukulura" to know someone, or something in and out to the extent of not being duped or tricked.

'*kulure*' is in reference to placing someone in one's hold. If repeated, '*kulure-kulure*' is in reference to the act of one being done and fixed.

"Mathangeni wakati wagwenthere umu na umu, kweni muvyala wake wali naye kulure/kulure-kulure mpaka wakoleka."

Kunchi[2]

This is from the verb "kukunchila" to cause to surge backwards – as with a car stopped suddenly, or to nod.

'*kunchi*' is in reference to the single act of surging backwards, or nodding. If repeated, '*kunchi-kunchi*' is in reference to repeated backward surges resulting from a sudden stop of a moving vehicle, or nods.

"Chifukwa cha kwimilila luwilo, galimoto yikachita kuti kunchi-kunchi."

"Malango pa kuzgola fumbo, wakachita waka mutu kunchi."

Kungumu[2]

This is from the verb "kukungumuka" to move about in a show-off manner with shoulders high, or to appear haughty.

'kungumu' is in reference to the act of showing off. If repeated, *'kungumu-kungumu'* is in reference to continued acts of showing off.

"Nkhuku-ndembu yati yawona nyatazi wake, mbwenu mahungwa kungumu."

"Wati wapulika kuti wakwela vilingwa, Nyokase, mbwenu pakwenda kungumu-kungumu."

Kunkhulu[2] or Kunkhule or Kunkhuliru

These come from the verbs "kukunkhula" or "kukunkhulira" to physically roll oneself over the ground, usually in supplication or humility.

'kunkhulu' or *'kunkhulire'* or *'kunkhuliru'* is in reference to the act of rolling over once. If repeated, *'kunkhulu-kunkhulu'* is in reference to to continuous acts of rolling over and over.

"Kulongola kuwonga kwake kwa fumu, mbwenu Sinya pasi kunkhulu/kunkhule/kunkhuliru/kunkhulu-kunkhulu.

Kunkhuzge[2]

This is derived from the verb "kukunkhuzga" to push – as with a pushbike when not ridden, or to cause to roll over ground – as with a cylinder.

'kunkhuzge' is in reference to a single act of rolling. If repeated, *'kukhuzge-kunkhuzge'* is in reference to several acts of rolling an object.

"Mafuta ghati ghamala mu galimoto, mbwenu Tumbikani na Jando galimoto yila kunkhuzge."

"Dango wati wawa pasi, mbwenu ŵanyake bali naye kunkhuzge-kunkhuzge mu dongo."

Kunyu

This comes from the verb "kukunyula" to pluck or pull off feathers.

'kunyu' is in reference to that detachment of feather from the skin.

"Apo nkhayezganga kuti nikole nkhuku, mbwenu mahungwa kunyu."

Kunyule[2]

This also comes from the verb 'kukunyula' to remove a bird's feathers.

'kunyule' is in reference to the act of removing feathers. If repeated, *'kunyule-kunyule'* is in reference to the removal of all feathers.

"Tati tayithila maji ghakocha, mbwenu nkuku yila kunyule/kunyule-kunyule."

Kusu²

'kusu' is in refence to a situation where an animal or person (usually large) is lying or resting. If repeated, *'kusu-kusu'* is in reference to more than one animal, or peson resting, or, in imagery, in reference to a healthy crop of pumpkins.

"Zovu yachita kuti kusu mu munda wa Zonde."

"Nkharamu zachita kuti kusu-kusu mudambo zati zalya boli."

"Mathanga ghachita kuti kusu-kusu mu munda wa Soyaphi."

Kwakwalizge

This is from the verb "kukwakwalizga" to hastily lift off an object from the ground – as with a crow picking a morsel of food.

'kwakwalizge' is the act of quickly lifting off an object and running off with it.

"Apo Phyokani wakaŵa kuti watangwanika mu sitolo yake, mbwenu Zikani tu matambala uto tukaŵa pa thebulo kwakwalizge."

Kwamphu

This comes from the verb "kukwamphula" to snatch, or to collect hurriedly.

'kwamphu' is in reference to the act of quickly snatching something from a holder.

"Uko Mabuchi wakuti wambe kulya yembe, mbweu Chawezi wali nayo kwamphu."

Kwaniske² (see "fiske")

This is from the verb "kukwaniska" or "kukwaniliska" to meet an obligation, or to satisfy, or to complete successfully.

'kwaniske' is in reference to finishing or meeting the obligation. If repeated, *'kwanise-kwanise'* is in reference to meeting all requirements.

"Nanga uli ŵanthu ŵakaghanaghananga kuti wamalenge chara, mbwenu Wanangwa nchito yose yila kwaniske/kwaniske-kwaniske."

Kwanjamu

This is from the verb 'kukwanjamuka" to stand out – as with ears of a dog when alarmed.

'*kwanjamu*' is in reference to ears standing out, or positioned upwards as an antenna. Euphemistically '*kwanjamu*' has been used when to denigrate a person's ears – if seen to resemble an antenna.

"Tikamanya kuti tili pa fupi na ulwani tati tawona galu makuti kuti kwanjamu."

"Awonani Malopa – makutu ghakuchita kuti kwanjamu!"

Kwanju

This comes from the verb "kukwanjula" to cut off a pieace without due care.

'*kwanju*' refers to the act of cutting off.

"Dumisani chisulo cha ŵene mbwenu dala kwanju!"

Kwee[3]

This comes from the verb "kukwekweta" to pull an object along a surface.

'*kwee*' is in reference to a single pull. If tripled, *"kwee-kwee-kwee"* refers to a prolonged drag of some object – as in pulling along a log of wood.

"Nanga uli wakakanizgika, mbwenu Kondwani chitete chila kwe-kwe-kwe."

Kwekwete[2]

This is also from the verb "kukwekweta" to pull along, or to drag along, or to tow.

'*kwekwete*" is in reference to a single act of dragging or towing. If repeated, '*kwekwete-kwekwete*' is in reference to more than one drag.

"Mumalo wwakuti wathwike pa mutu, mbwenu chitete chila kwekwete/kwekwete-kwekwete pasi."

Kwemu

This comes from the verb "kukwemula" to bruise brutally.

'*kwemu*' is in reference to that heavy friction resulting in loss of skin.

"Kumbukani wakawa uheni mpaka khongono kwemu."

Kwenyu

This comes from the verb "kukwenyula" to tear away a piece of meat – as tearing a wing from a chicken.

'*kwenyu*' refers to the detachment of the small piece from the main body.

"Uko Chinga wakukuntha nkhuku, mbwenu chikumba nacho kwenyu chifukwa chakocha kwa maji."

Kwinyililu² or Kwinyilile²

These come from the verb "kukwinyilira" to be stunted, or not growing with strength, or to suffer in silence – as with a human.

'kwinyililu' or 'kwinyilile' is in reference to an indication of stunted growth, or an indication of suffering in silence. If repeated, *'kwinyililu-kwinyililu'* or *'kwinyilile-kwinyilile'* is in reference to the inability to walk about with energy, or move about because of severe malnutrition or severe suffering.

"Chifukwa cha chilala, mbuto zose mu munda mbwenu kwinyililu/kwinyililu-kwinyililu pa kumela."

"Mwamuwona Chimwemwe ku maso wachita kuti kwinyilile/kwinyilile-kwinyilile chifukwa cha urwiri mu nthumbo."

Kwinyimbu²

This is derived from the verbs "kukwinyimbula" to distort one's face (maybe because of pain) or the verb "kukwinyimbuka" to be distorted in the face (as when about to cry).

'kwinyimbu' is in reference to the act of distorting one's face as one is about to cry. If repeated, *'kwinyimbu-kwinyimbu'* refers to more than one act of facial distortion.

"Ŵati ŵamuthyapula Chigomezgo, mbwenu ku maso kwinyimbu/kwinyimbu-kwinyimbu."

Kwipi

'kwipi' is in reference to total penetration, or entry up to the hilt.

"Pakaŵa kuti wangapona chala – mukondo ukanjila wose kwipi mwa Lazalo."

Kwiti

'kwiti' is in reference to an instantaneous swarming of a crowd onto an object – as with flies onto a piece of bad meat, or an angry mob onto a thief.

"Wezi wati fike waka pa kaya, mbwenu twana kwiti."

Kwizu or Kwizule

These are derived from the verb "kukwizula" to pull one's dress up with the object of exposing one self.

'*kwizu*' or '*kwizule*' is the act of pulling up one's clothes or dress to expose the body.

"Mzamose wati wafika pa mulonga, mbwenu siketi yake kwizu/kwizule."

Lakalaka

This comes from the verb "kulakaska" to cause fruit to drop through shaking the tree.

'*laka-laka*' could be in reference to the falling of fruit, or the dropping of tears, or rain, or falling off of termite soil covering a tree.

"Ŵati ŵasukunya khuni, mbwenu masuku lakalaka."

"Siyenji wati wapulika za yifwa, mbwenu masozi lakalaka."

Lalawu (also see "gagawu")

This comes from the verb "kulalawula" to peel, or to remove skin by peeling – as when removing gauze stuck to a wound, or breaking skin when whipped.

'*lalawu*' refers to that process of peeling or the opening of skin in response to a whip (also see '*gagawu*').

"Apo tikawuskangapo bandeji pa chilonda, mbwenu na chikumba wuwo lalawu."

Lamatu (also see "lalawu")

This is from the verb "kulamatula" to peel something glued or attached to another object – as with a puncture patch, or from the verb "kulamatuka" to be unstuck.

'*lamatu*' refers to the dislodging of something stuck to something else.

"Wati wafundiska ku moto, mbwenu chigamba chila lamatu."

Landalanda

This is from the verb "kulandama" to lean forwards, or stoop.

'*landalanda*' is in reference to the act of stooping.

"Agogo sono pakwenda ni landalanda."

Langalanga

This comes from the verb "kulangala" to lack density, or to lack thick texture.

'langalanga' is in reference to seeing through, or the lack of adequate cover.

"Umo zinyifwa zatutizgila, zaleka chikaya langalanga."

"Makuni mu Chikangawa ghamala – awonani sono mukuchita kuti langalanga."

"Sokayawo wakuti wavwala, kweni awonani malaya ghakuchita kuti langalanga."

Lange²

This comes from the verb 'kulanga' to counsel, or to punish.

'lange' is in reference to the act of counseling, or punishing. If repeated, *'lange-lange'* is in reference to prolonged acts of counselling, or punishing.

"Chigomezgo wati wabuda, asambizgi mbwenu mwana yula lange."

"Tapiwa wati wamala msinkhu, mbwenu womama mwana yula lange-lange."

Langike²

This is from the verb "kulangika" to be counselled, or to be punished.

'langike' is in reference to being counselled once or punished once. If repeated, *'langike-langike'* is in reference to having been thouroughly counseled, or thoroughly punished.

"Siyenji wati wakula, mbwenu langike na womama."

"Kondwani wati wanjila mu gadi, mbwenu langike-langike."

Lefu²

This comes from the verb "kulefuka" to be without energy – as with someone hungry and thirty, or someone who is very ill.

'lefu' is in reference to the weak posture, or stooping posture because of lack of energy. If repeated, *'lefu-lefu'* is in reference to being without energy.

"Manyi nchifukwa cha njala, Chiyezgo wachita kuti lefu/lefu-lefu pa kwenda."

Legheleghe

This comes from the verb 'kuleghelezga' to tie loosely.

'legheleghe' refers to that looseness, or lack of tightness – as with a loose belt around the waist.

"Chifukwa kabunthu wakaŵa musani mu chiuno, mwana wati wavwala, mbwenu kabunthu legheleghe."

Leghelezge

This is from the verb "kuleghelezga" to hang something loosely or temporarily – as with placing an unfixed rafter on a beam.

'leghelezge' is in reference to the act of leaving something hanging loosely.

"Penjani wati wajintha nchindamila zake, mbwenu mgololo pachanya leghelezge."

Leke

This is from the verb "kuleka" to stop, or to let go, or desist.

'leke' is in reference to the act of stoping, desisting, or letting go.

"Ŵati ŵamulanga, mbwenu mwana yula nkhalo yiheni yila leke."

Lekelele[2]

This is from the verb "kulekelela" to deny someone guidance, or to pay little attention to norms.

'lekelele' is in reference to the act of ignoring guidance. If repeated, *'lekelele-lekelele'* is in reference to acts of total neglect.

"Chifukwa chakuti Mayengiso awiske ŵakamutemwanga chomene, mbwenu mwana yula lekelele mwakuti sono walije nchindi kwa waliyose."

"Yesaya munda mbwenu lekelele-lekelele mwakuti sono muli utheka wekha-wekha."

Lekelezge

This is from the verb "kulekelezga" to let go midway, or to suddenly stop an on-going process or activity, or to abandon – as with a child left unattended.

'lekekelezge' is in reference to the act of temporarily stopping from proceeding with an activity, or temporarily leaving a child unattended.

"Wati wapulika kupoma kwa vula, mbwenu Chiyezgo nchito yila lekelezge."

"Kumbukani wati wapulika kuti ŵanyina ŵafika, mbwenu mwana uyo wakaŵa mumawoko pasi lekelezge."

Lekezge

This is from the verb "kulekezga" to stop or to pause an activity before completion.

'lekezge' is in reference to the act of stopping or pausing an activity (permanently or temporarily).

"Chifukwa chakukalipilika, mbwenu Mazaza nchito yila lekezge."

Lengendu

This comes from the verb "kulengendula" to hit severely, or to shatter.

'lengendu' is in reference to a hard smash.

"Apo Masozi wakati wayezge kuzgolako, mbwenu Soyaphi wali naye lengendu."

Lepelepe

This is from the verb "kulepeska" to defecate or to drop in mass.

'lepelepe' is in reference to the falling out of some mass – as with an animal's dung, or intenstines falling out.

"Chimbwe wakachiluskika mpaka mavi lepelepe."

"Sangulukani wakatimba kalulu na mbavi mpaka matumbo lepelepe."

Lepete

This is from the verb "kulepeteka" to fall out in mass.

'lepete' is in reference to the falling out of some mass – as in animal dung, or intestines.

"Ng'ombe ŵakaitema munthumbo mpaka matumbo lepete kuwalo."

Lepete[2]

This is from the verb "kulepetuka" to lack rigidity in an organ.

'lepete' is in reference to the lack of life in an organ. If repeated, *'lepete-lepete'* is in reference to continued signs of lack of life in an organ.

"Mwamuwona Lazalo, milomo yachita kuti lepete."

"Mwana muchoko yula – kwene mabele ghali lepete."

"Mbachi pakwenda, mawoko ni lepete-lepete" or "lepetu-lepetu."

Lepwete[2]

This comes from the verb "kulepwetuka" to be loose, or not tight, or to be without strength or energy.

'lepwete" or 'lepwetu' is in reference to indications of lack of fitting – as with clothing, or lack of energy – as in a person whose body cannot hold straight. If repeated, *'lepwete-lepwete'* is in reference to either movements that show no energy, or clothing not fitting.

"Chifukwa chakughanda, Chiukepo sono vyakuvwala vikuchita kuti lepwete/lepwetu mu thupi.

"Chifukwa cha kulwala nyengo yitali, Chananga sono pakwenda ni lepwete/lepwete-lepwete."

Lewelewe

This is from the verb "kuleweleska" to tie loosely.

'lewelewe' is in reference to a scenario of something not tight – as with a pair of trousers that is over-size in the waist, or as with a door handle that is loose. Euphemistically, it could be in reference to moral decay, or the lack of integrity.

"Chifukwa cha kuvunda kwa mathabwa ghamumphepete, chijalo chili lewelewe."

"Musungwana yula, nkhalo ni lewelewe."

Lifu

This is from the verb "kulifuka" to bend over, or to fail to remain upright.

'lifu' is in reference to the inability of remaining upright.

"Mapesi mwana nimutali – pakwenda wakuchita kuti lifu."

"Chifukwa cha jumi, utheka wachita kuti lifu."

Likhe[2]

This is from the verb " kulikha" to fell.

'likhe' is in reference to the act of felling. If repeated, *'likhe-likhe'* is in reference to felling trees (or humans) over a large area.

"Nanga uli ŵakamukanizga, mbwenu ku usiku Soyaphi khuni lila likhe."

"Awonani Saulosi – makuni ghose mu munda mbwenu likhe-likhe."

Likiti or Likitu

This comes from the verb "kulikita" to hit severely - usually with a stick.

'likiti' or *'likitu'* refers to the the act of thumping.

"Uko Lazalo wakuti wachimbile, Mafunase wali naye likiti/likitu na m'bada."

Likitike[2]

This comes from the verb "kulikitika" to be severely beaten, or to be hit to pulp, or to lose one's body due to illness.

'likitike' is in reference to receiving blows and being subdued, or in reference to one being subdued due to a serious illness.

"Apo Zakeyo wakakhumbanga kuthaska munyake, iye naye mbwenu likitike/likitike-likitike."

"Utenda wati wamusanga, mbwenu Soyaphi likitike/likitike-likitike."

Limaze[2]

This is from the verb "kulimaza" to maim or to cripple.

'limaze' is in reference to a single act of maimimg or crippling a living thing. If repeated, *'limaze-limaze'* is in reference to total maiming or crippling of a live object.

"Mbachi mwanakazi wake wakutowa yula mbwenu limaze/limaze-limaze chifukwa cha kumutimba nyengo na nyengo."

Lindimu (also see "wundumu")

This comes from the verb "kulindimula" to crush, or to pull down – as with a wall, or the verb "kulindimuka" to collapse – also as with a wall.

'lindimu' refers to the disintegration, or the falling of the wall as it is being pulled down.

"Vula yati yamala waka, mbwenu chiliŵa nacho lindimu."

Lipwiti

This is derived from the verb "kulipwitika" to be soft in texture, or to appear weak – as with a leaf, or piece of cloth that has lost its vibrancy.

'lipwiti' is in reference to the feel of lack of texture or stamina in an object.

"Manyi nchifukwa cha kocha, mahamba ghachita kuti lipwiti."

"Malaya ghachita kuti lipwiti chifukwa chakumala."

Litu

This comes from the verb "kulituka" to be over-burdened – as with a branch laden with fruit, or eye lids that are full of sleep.

'litu' is in reference to the over abundance of fruit on a branch, or as with eyes that fail to remain open because of sleep.

"Masuku ghachita kuti litu mukhuni."

"Chifukwa cha kuchezela, tulo tuchali litu mumaso Lazalo."

Lizu

This is from the verb "kulizula" to tear off skin on impact – as when boot studs scrape someone's skin.

'lizu' is in reference to the coming off of skin on impact.

"Tiyezge wakawa mpaka makongono ghose lizu."

Loli

This is from the verb "kulolotela" to be absent minded, or to day-dream.

'loli' is in reference to the act of staring blankly, or being absent minded.

"Awonani Zikani wati waka loli."

Lolophu

This comes from the verb "kululophola" to pull out something long from under a cover.

'lolophu' is in reference to the act of pulling out something long and having it exposed.

"Njoka yati yafwa kukhululu, mbwenu Soyaphi wali nayo lolophu."

Loloŵala²

This comes from the verb "kuloloŵala" to move slowly and without energy. If repeated, *'loloŵala-loloŵala'* is in reference to the act of walking or moving slowly and without strength.

"Jika pakwenda sono wakuchita kuti loloŵala/loloŵala-loloŵala chifukwa cha utenda."

Lomboto

This comes from the verb "kulombotoka" to lack stiffness, or firmness, or energy, or life – as in grass hit by drought, or as in a person's body subjected to illness, or as in under-cooked sima.

'lomboto' refers to the state of lack of energy or firmness.

"Pala sima yindaphye, yikuchita kuti lomboto mumawoko."

"Ngoma zachita kuti lomboto muminda chifukwa sono sabata njachitatu vula yindawe."

Londo²

This comes from the verb "kulondola" to follow.

'londo' refers to the act of stalking, or following. If repeated, *'londo-londo'* is in reference to motions of following, or stalking an object everywhere they go.

"Tiwonge ncheŵe yake yikumutemwa – pose apo wakwenda ni londo/londo-londo."

Longole²

This is from the verb "kulongola" to point out, or to show, or to expose.

'longole' is the act of pointing, showing, or exposing. If repeated, *'longole-longole'* is usually in reference to the act of exhibiting, or exposing secret things without reservations.

"Ŵanthu ŵati ŵafumba nthowa, mbwenu Kondwani nthowa yila longole."

"Nanga uli tikabisa katundu, Malizgani mbwenu katundu yula longole-longole kwa mafumu."

Lopoto (also see "lomboto")

This comes from the verb "kulopotoka" to have no strength, or to feel physically weak.

'lopoto' is in reference to being weak.

"Mwamuwona Mbateta pakugwila nchito – mawoko ghakuchita kuti lopoto."

"Nozgechi nayo pakugwila nchito ni lopoto-lopoto."

Lothya

'lothya' is in reference to the stoop of a male organ, or the stoop in an animal's tail.

"Mchila wa nkhalamu wachita kuti lothya."

Loto

This comes from the verb "kulotoka" or "kusotoka" – to charge.

'loto' is in reference to the act of charging – as with an angry dog.

"Uko tichali kunozgeka na vyakulwera, mbwenu nkhalamu loto."

Loto^2

This is from the verb "kulotoka" to die off – as with a fire, or anger.

'loto' is in reference to a fire, or anger dying off. If repeated, *'loto-loto'* is in reference to fire almost dead, or the calming down of anger.

"Tati tazelezga kusonkha moto, mbwenu moto wula loto."

"Mukati mu usiku, mbwenu moto nawo loto-loto."

"Mazaza ŵati ŵamukhazika pasi madoda, mbwenu ukali nawo loto-loto."

Lulumalu

This is from the verb "kululumala" to sit in a drooping posture, or to slouch – may be because of grief or illness.

'lulumalu' is in reference to one's body slouching and being without spirit, or exuberance.

"Yesaya wati waka lulumalu pa nyumba chifukwa cha kulwalalwala."

Lwaha (also see "zeza")

This is from the noun "chilwaha" loss of attentiveness, or concentration, or day-dreaming.

'lwaha' is in reference to appearing blank, or at a loss, or appearing confused when confronted with truth, or simply day-dreaming.

"Madazi ghano, Yezgani pali pose apo wakhala, mbwenu ni lwaha."

"Jando ŵati ŵamupanikizga na unenesko, mbwenu lwaha."

Malizge

This is from the verb "kumalizga" to finish, or to complete.

'malizge' is in reference to the act of completing.

"Uko Muwuso na Chigomezgo ŵakusuŵilila kuseŵela, mbwenu Tawomga nchito iyo ŵakamupa malizge."

Malizgike

This is from the verb "kumalizgika" to breathe the last breath – or to die.

'malizgike' is in reference to the fleeting breath in death, or the passing of the last breath.

"Apo tikayezganga kumugadabula, mbwenu mulwali yula malizgike."

Matu

This is from the verb "kumatula" to separate something stuck to another.

'matu' is in reference to the removal of something with adhesive – as with a puncture patch.

"Tati tafundiskapo na moto, mbwenu chigamba chila matu."

Mazge

This is from the verb "kumazga" to break-up – as with a contract, or to end a relationship, or to divorce.

'mazge' refers to the act of breaking-up, or closing off a relationship.

"Zakeyo wati wapulika waka kuti mwanakazi wake wakwenda uheni, mbwenu nthengwa yila mazge."

Mbe

'*mbe*' is the act of biting.

"Uko wakonkha, mbwenu Chigomezgo wali nalo bele la ŵanyina mbe."

Mbete or Mbetu

This is from the verb "kumbeteska" to off-load in huge amounts – as with animal feaces.

'*mbete*' or '*mbetu*' is in reference to the splash down of mass. If repeated, '*mbete-mbete*' or '*mbetu –mbetu*' is in reference to dropping mass more than once.

"Ng'ombe yikafyenyeka mpaka mavi mbete/mbetu/mbete-mbete."

Mbii or Mbinini

This is from the verbs "kumbiniska" to scatter, or "kumbininika" to be scattered.

'*mbii*' or '*mbinini*' is in reference to the motions of being scattered in all directions.

"Nkharamu yati yafika, mbwenu ng'ombe mbii/mbinini."

Mbindingu

This comes from the verb "kumbindingula" to reverse a process.

'*mbindingu*" is in reference to the act of suddenly turning over, or suddenly reversing a process.

"Apo tose tikaghanaghananga kuti tili pamoza mumaghanoghano, mbwenu Soyaphi mbindingu."

"Tati tafika pa Ruviri, mbwenu galimoto yila mbindingu."

Mbo

This comes from the verb "kumbonya" to cover a large area – as with rain over an area, or a tarpaulin over a truck.

'*mbo*' is in reference to total coverage of an object or area.

"Apo tikati tambepo ulendo wa kusukulu, mbwenu vula nayo mbo."

Mboto[2]

This is from the verb "kumbotoska" or "kumbotoka" to drop.

'mboto' is in reference to the dropping down of something. If repeated, *'mboto-mboto'* is in reference to lot more objects dropping.

"Apo Dango wakaŵikanga ndalama mu thumba mwake, mbwenu ndalama yila pasi mboto."

"Thumba lati ladoloka, mbwenu ndalama nazo mboto-mboto."

Mbu³

'mbu' is in reference to a container being full; *'mbu-mbu-mbu'* is in reference to a container being over-filled.

"Chihengo chazula mbu."

"Chitete chazula mbu-mbu-mbu na vingoma."

Mbwa

'mbwa' is in reference to the act of suddenly meeting or running into someone, or running into each other.

"Apo Thumbiko wakachimbilanga, mbwenu na Lazalo mbwa panthowa."

Mbwakambwaka (also see "katakata")

This is from the verb "kumbwambwantha" to shiver, or to tremble – as because of cold or fear.

'mbwakambwaka" is the act of shivering.

"Ŵati ŵamumanga unyolo, mbwenu Chandiwira mbwakambwaka."

Mbwa-mbwa-mbwa

This is also from the verb "kumbwambwantha" to shiver.

'mbwa-mbwa-mbwa' is in reference either to the act of shivering, or in reference to the expression of joy or appreciation because of an unexpected favour, or event – as when unexpectedly freed from incarceration, or when receiving a valuable gift.

"Mwana wakuchita kuti mbwa-mbwa-mbwa chifukwa cha kuzizima."

"Nyambose wakachita kuti mbwa-mbwa-mbwa wati wapokela thumba la vingoma."

Mbwee or Mbwerere

This is from the verb 'kumbwerereska" to spread objects, or to produce in abundance.

'mbwee' or *'mbwerere'* is in reference to things or objects being all over, or in plenty.

"Munyumba ya Mbachi, vinthu ni mbwee/mbwerere naumo muwoli wake wali kufumilapo."

"Panyumba ya Ŵasekulu, vyakulya ni mbwee/mbwerere."

Mbwefu

This is from the verb "kumbwefula" to throw someone down – as in a fight.

'mbwefu' is in reference to the landing of an object being thrown off.

"Apo Mwiza wakasambilanga kukwela njinga, yikamuwiska uko mbwefu."

Mbwi[3]

'mbwi' is in reference to defecating, but in small piles.

'mbwi-mbwi-mbwi' is in reference to defecating in small quantities or piles and scattered all over.

"Ŵati ŵamukhizga ku musana, mbwenu mwana yula mavi pasi mbwi."

"Mwana wati waluta kuseli kwa nyumba, mbwenu mavi pali pose mbwi-mbwi-mbwi."

Memene[2]

This is from the verb "kumemena" to chew a hard object, or to bite off pieces from an unripe fruit using bare teeth.

'memene' is in reference to a single bite or a single chip into an unripe fruit. If repeated, *'memene-memene'* is in reference to several bites or chips into somethingt using bare teeth.

"Wati wapaula yembe mu khuni, mbwenu yembe yila memene."

"Ncheŵe yati yasola chiwangwa, mbwenu chiwangwa chila memene-memene."

Meng'enyu[2]

This is from the verb "kumeng'enyula" to bounce one's buttocks.

'meng'enyu' is in reference to a single movement of muscle. If repeated, *'meng'enyu-meng'enyu'* is in reference to several bounces of muscles.

"Nkhuzi yakwithu linunda likuchita kuti meng'enyu pala yikwenda."

"Tafwa pakwenda, nyuma yose yikuchita kuti meng'enyu-meng'enyu."

Menye or Menyu

This is from the verb "kumenya" either to slice off a morsel using one's palm, or to split an object with the use of bare hands into two or more pieces.

'menye' or *'menyu'* is in reference to the act of taking a morsel, or splitting an object. If repeated, *'menye-menye'* is in reference to breaking mass into small bits.

"Wati wageza mawoko, mbwenu sima yila menye nakwamba kukonya."

"Chingoma chati chaphya, mbwenu menye-menye kuti ŵana wose ŵakwane ."

Mete² or Metu²

This is from the verb "kumeta" to shave.

'mete' or *'metu'* is in reference to a single stroke of shaving. If repeated, *'mete-mete'* is in reference to continuous acts of shaving.

"Uko mwana wachali mutulo, mbwenu sisi lila mete/metu."

"Tati tasunga thupi, mbwenu sisi zithu mete-mete."

'metu-metu' however, is often in reference to the rising of one's hair, or the feeling of having things moving through one's hair because of being scared.

"Ndati njile waka kuthondo, mbwenu sisi lane metu-metu, ndipo nyengo yeneyiyo nkhawelela."

Mimite²

This is from the verb "kumimita" to remove particles or debris from the surface of a drink through a slow sip.

'mimite' is in reference to the act of a single sip. If repeated, *'mimite-mimite'* is in reference to several acts of sipping and having a thorough clean-up of the unwanted particles or debris in the drink.

"Mumalo mwakuti wauskemo tuviswaswa muchindongwa na kakhuni, mbwenu chindongwa chila mimite/mimite-mimite na mulomo nakuthunya tuviswaswa tula."

Monkho

This is from the verb "kumonkhola" to dislodge, or to demolish.

'monkho' is in reference to dislodging.

"Chakufwa wakatimba muwoli wakhe pa mulomo mpaka jino monkho."

Mphwa (also see "mwaa")

'mphwa' is is in reference to the feeling of nausea.

"Tapona wati wamwa mankhwala, mbwenu mtima mphwa."

Mwaa

This is from the verb "kumwazika" to feel sick at heart, or indignant

'mwaa' is in reference to that sudden feeling of indignation at heart, or that sudden feeling of sickness.

"Wati wamanya kuti Soyaphi yekha ndiye wapokelenge njombe, mbwenu Lazalo mtima mwaa."

"Mbachi wati wamemena musekese, mbwenu mtima mwaa."

Mwe-mwe-mwe

This is derived from the verb "kumwemwetela" to break into a smile – as in showing joy, amusement or friendliness.

'mwe-mwe-mwe' is in reference to the act of turning up of the corners of the mouth and breaking into a smile showing pleasure or joy – as when receiving a loved one.

"Wezi wati waniwona waka, mbwenu mwe-mwe-mwe."

Mwetu

This is from the verb "kumwetula" to flash as in an approaching storm or the verb "kumwetulila" also to break into a short smile.

'mwetu' is in reference to that sudden flash of light, or that sudden appearance of a smile. Sometimes it can also be used in reference to the sudden appearance of someone unexpected.

"Vula yati yamba waka kulokwa, mbwenu leza mwetu."

"Towela wati wandiwona, mbwenu naye mwetu."

"Uko tichali kuyowoya za kuchedwa kwa Thumbiko, mbwenu naye mwetu."

Myaa

'myaa' is in reference to a state of peace or calm, or bliss.

"Panyumba ya ŵasekulu pali myaa nyengo yose."

Myange² or Myangu

This stems from the verb "kumyanga" to lick, or to pass the tongue over one's lips.

'myange' or *'myangu'* are in reference to that movement of the tongue over lips or surface of something.

"Wuchi wati wamuthikila mumawoko, mbwenu Tumbikani mawoko ghala myange/myangu/myange-myange."

Myangulizge

This is from the verb "kumyangulizga" to lick one's lips because of having eaten or taken something likeable.

'myangulizge' is in reference to the act of cleaning ones lips with one's tongue after eating or taking something tasty.

"Nyembezi wati wamala kulya sima ya nkhuku yila, mbwenu milomo myangulizge."

Namphwinamphwi (also see "bwitu-bwitu")

This is from the verb "kunamphwila" to be oozy – as with some wild fruits when ripe (matowo).

'namphwinamphwi' is in reference to the greasy appearance of an object because of too much ooze or oil.

"Kuseli kwa nyumba yakwithu, matowo ghakuchita kuti namphwinamphwi."

"Awonani Suzgika – kumaso kukuchita kuti namphwinamphwi mafuta."

Natu²

This is from the verb "kunata" to be sticky – as when covered by some adhesive substance.

'natu' is in reference to that feel of something sticky. If repeated, *'natu-natu'* is in reference to the persistent feel of a sticky substance – maybe because of humidity, dirt, sweat, or grease.

"Pala phula lafunda, likuchita kuti natu."

"Chifukwa chakuleka kugeza, Chananga pa msana ni natu-natu."

Nche-nche

'nche-nche' is in reference to the act of being ill-at-ease and constantly casting furtive glances around oneself.

"Chidongo wamba mbele kuti nche-nche – manyi wakopachi!"

Ndendende

'ndendende' is in reference to being exactly similar – as in appearance or behaviour, or in reference to fitting exactly into something – as into a pair of shoes, or dress, or being full to the brim.

"Mwana uyu wakozga ŵawiske ndendende."

"Skapato zamukwana Malango ndendende."

"Sinthani wazuzga chidundu chake ndendende."

Ndindandinda

This is from the verb "kundinda" to be without, or to panic in the absence of support.

'ndindandinda' is in reference to the coming on of signs of panic – as when confronted by guests when not ready for them, or as with the sudden loss of shelter or support.

Ŵalendo ŵati ŵafika, mbwenu Lazalo ndindandinda chifukwa cha kuŵevye vyakudika."

"Ŵawiskewo ŵati ŵatayika, mwenu ŵana ndindandinda."

Ndi-ndi-ndi

'ndi-ndi-ndi' is in reference to the scenario of a large number of people gathered together.

"Pa yifwa ya Mkakeni, ŵanthu ŵakachita kuti ndi-ndi-ndi."

Ndo

'ndo' is in reference to the feel of weight – the feel that the object is heavy. It could also be used figuratively to denote status or wealth.

"Thanga liweme likuti ndo mumawoko."

"Munyinu yula ngwa ndo – mungamuseweleskanga!"

Ndu

'ndu' is in reference to something being in a heap.

"Paseli pa nyumba pali mavi ndu."

Ndwii

'ndwii' is in reference to an atmosphere of gloom – as in a stormy sky, or as one in a bad mood.

"Muhanya uno kundache makola – kuwalo kwachita kuti ndwii."

"Nyasinga nyengo zose kukhala kwake ni ndwii."

Neghe (also see "teke")

This comes from the verb "kunegha" to draw – as in water from a well.

'neghe' is in reference to the act of drawing or taking from a source.

"Lumbani wati wanjila mu nyumba, mbwenu maji ghake neghe pambele wandakhale pasi."

Neng'enezge

This is from the verb "kuneng'enezga" to tie loosely – as with a loose noose around a neck or to leave hanging loosely.

'neng'enezge' is in reference to the act of leaving a loop or noose loose or leaving an object hanging loosely.

"Wati wakola mbuzi yake, mbwenu chingwe mu singo neng'enezge."

"Soyaphi wati wanjila mu nyumba, mbwenu chipewa chake neng'enezge pa muzumali."

Ng'anamu

This is from the verb "kung'anamuka" to turn round.

'ng'anamu' is in reference to the act of physically turning round, or is in reference to the act of suddenly switching sides, or refuting a position already agreed upon.

"Zalerapi wati wamugunyuzga Sinya, mbwenu Sinya ng'anamu."

"Apo tikatenge tose tili pamoza, mbwenu munyithu ng'anamu."

Ng'anu

This is from the verb "kung'anuzga" or "kung'anula" to push forcibly or to push off.

'ng'anu' is in refrerence to the act of pushing off something forcibly.

"Ŵati ŵakhala pa mzele, mbwenu Tasokwa wali nayo Ndagha ng'anu."

Ng'azi²

This is from the verb "kung'azima" to glitter.

'ng'azi' is in reference to the glitter. If repeated, *'ng'azi-ng'azi'* is in reference to continuous glittering.

"Maria wati waphaka mafuta mbwenu chisko ng'azi."

"Phyoka lundi likatupa mpaka ng'azi-ng'azi."

Ng'oli

This is from the verb "kung'ola" to deride someone by gesture, and usually from the backside.

'ng'oli' is in reference to the act of gesturing in derision.

"Mwanuwona Zeleza – apo wakhala mbwenu nchito ni ng'oli kwa ŵanyake ."

Ng'ondo

This is from the verb "kung'ondola" or "kung'ondoska" to cause to scatter.

'ng'ondo' is in reference to the act of being scattered.

"Ng'ombe zati zachiluskika na nkhalamu, mbwenu ng'ondo."

Ng'onomu

This is from the verb "kung'onomola" or "kung'onomoka" to slide down.

'ng'onomu' is in reference to the act of sliding or slipping down. Euphemistically, it can be in reference to dying.

"Tapona wati wasezga figha limoza, mbwenu nkhali nayo ng'onomu."

"Uko tikuchezga naye munyithu muchipatala, mbwenu munthu yula ng'onomu."

Ng'ozo

This is from the verb "kung'ozoka" to fall and land with the nose first.

'ng'ozo' is in reference to the impact of the nose hitting the ground.

"Chandiwira ŵakamukanchizga mpaka pasi ng'ozo."

Ng'ulung'uze[2]

This is derived from the verb "kung'ulung'uza" to gnaw, or to chew off all tissue from a bone.

'ng'ulung'uze" is in reference to the act of gnawing or chewing tissue off from bone. If repeated, *'ng'ulung'uze-ng'ulung'uze'* is in reference to the act of completely cleaning-out tissue from bone.

"Timeyo wati wamala kulya, mbwenu chiwanga chila ng'ulung'uze'/ng'ulung'uze-ng'ulung'uze."

Ngundangunda

'ngundangunda' is in reference to lots of animals, pumpkins, or humans lying together.

"Mathanga ghachita kuti ngundangunda mu munda."

"Tikasanga vigwele vili ngundangunda pa dambo."

Ng'ung'une[2]

This comes from the verb "kung'ung'una" also to gnaw, or to chew a bone clean.

'ng'ung'une' is in reference to a single act of gnawing. If repeated *'ng'ung'une-ng'ung'une'* is in reference to several acts of chewing and cleaning a bone.

"Wati walya nyama, mbwenu chiwangwa nacho ng'ung'une/ng'ung'une-ng'ung'une."

Ngwanju

This is from the verb "kungwanjula" to chop off – as by using a panga.

'ngwanju' is in reference to the act of chopping off and actually removing a part.

"Uko Mapesi wakusolola thabwa, mbwenu Suzgo thabwa lila ngwanju dala."

Ngwee

This is from the verb "kungweluka" to lighten up – as in the coming of dawn, or as with skies clearing up, or the verb "kungweluska" to enlighten.

'ngwee' is in reference to brightening, or clearing, or that the situation is clear.

"Magesi ghati ghafika, mbwenu mu nyumba mose ngwee."

"Yesaya wati walongosola suzgo lake, mbwenu tose mitima ngwee."

Ning'ining'i

This is from the verb "kuning'inizga" to make the middle narrow.

'ning'ining'i' is in reference to appearing narrow in the middle – as with a wasp's waste.

"Awonani Tabita – pa chiwuno pakuchita kuti ning'iningi."

Ning'inizge

This is also from the verb "kuning'inizga" to make the middle thin.

'ning'inizge' is in reference to the act of thinning a part of an object.

"Apo Nchindi wakaŵajanga ndodo yake, mbwenu pakati na pakati ning'inizge."

Njizge/njizgu

This is from the verb "kunjizga" to penetrate, or to force a way into – as with the male organ into the female organ – or a ball into a goal.

'njizge/njizgu' is in reference to the act of inserting.

"Chidongo wati watola phesulo, mbwenu mu mphuno njizge/njizgu."

Nkha

This is from the noun "nkhanya" a taste that is sour.

'nkha' is in reference to a sour taste – as with an unripe fruit. Euphemistically, it can also be applied to an individual's attitude or mood.

"Pala munthu walya thyokolo lambula kupya, mumulomo namo ni nkha."

"Thokozani mumutole makola – mwana yula ngwa nkha."

Nong'onong'o (also see "tapitapi")

This is from the verb "kunong'omela" to be excessively sweet – as with pure honey.

'nong'onong'o' is in reference to the feeling of utmost sweetness throughout the body or in the mouth.

"Yembe za kamunowa zikuchita kuti nong'onong'o pala ukulya."

"Umo nakhalira pa zuwa, thupi lose likuchita kuti nong'onong'o."

Nthonyezge[2]

This is from the verb "kunthonyezga" to squeeze a drop of some fluid into something – as with eye drops, or a drop of cooking oil into a pan.

'nthonyezge' is in reference to the act of squeezing a drop of some liquid into something – as into an eye, or into a pan. If repeated, *'nthonyezge-nthonyezge'* is in reference to squeezing several drops.

"Anyina ŵati ŵawona kuti mwana wakoleka na vimbokoli, mbwenu mankhwala mumaso mula nthonyezge/nthonyezge-nthonyezge."

Nu

'nu' is in reference to being incommunicado or not willing to say anything.

"Nanga uli nkhanyengo sono kumufumba, Tapona wachali nu."

Nuske

This is derived from the verb "kunuska" to sniff off or to smell through sniffing.

'nuske' is the act of sniffing.

"Mwamuwona Lusungu – kanandi pala wakugula sopo, mbwenu dankha sopo yila nuske."

Nwa

'nwa' is in reference to the act of suddenly and quickly capturing an object that was fleeing.

"Apo Zonde wakaghanaghananga za kuchimbila, ŵa polisi ŵali naye nwa."

Nwii

'nwii' is in reference to a feeling of pain through nerves.

"Namunyinu kawoko kamba kale kuti nwii – manyi ni nyamakazi?

Nya or Nya-nya

'*nya*' is is in reference to the act of sinking into soft substance – as with a vehicle into mud, or as with a leg into water, or simply in reference to depth – as with an open wound or pit. If repeated, however, '*nya-nya*' is in reference to the act of tiptoeing, or walking quietly with the heels off the ground.

"Tili pafupi kufika pa chkaya, mbwenu galimoto mu mathipa nya."

"Chilonda cha Lazalo chachita kuti nya."

"Ulanda wakachita kuti nya-nya pakwenda kopa chiwawa."

Nyang'ama

This is from the verb "kunyang'ama" to position oneself in an elevated position – as with a cooking pot over a fire.

'*nyang'ama*' is in reference either to the squatting position, or the elevation of the object.

"Mwamuwona Fumbamtima wachita kuti nyang'ama pa kampando!"

"Nkhali ya sima yachita kuti nyang'ama pa mafigha."

Nyang'amale

This is from the verb "kunyang'amala" to squat or to crouch with the knees bent.

'*nyang'amale*' is in reference to the act of squatting.

"Chiphwafu wati wafika pa madoda, mbwenu nyang'amale."

Nyaru

This is from the verb "kunyaruska" to cause to be plenty.

'*nyaru*' is in reference to things – or animals – being everywhere and in large numbers.

"Pa chikaya chakwithu, ŵana ŵakuchita kuti nyaru."

Nyeketu

This is from the verb "kunyeketula" to melt or "kunyeketuka" to be melted.

'*nyeketu*' is in reference to melting.

"Mphika wati wapya, mbwenu mafuta gha nyama nagho nyeketu."

"Tati tathila maji ghanandi, mbwenu dongo lila nyeketu."

Nyelemu[2]

This is from the verb "kunyelemuka" to move off smoothly and quietly, or to slide off smoothly – as with a car on a slope, or as with water out of one's palm.

'nyelemu' is in reference to that quiet exit, or take off, or the loss of liquid from one's palm. If repeated, *'nyelemu-nyelemu'* is in reference to the slow but quiet movement of a car or fluid.

"Ŵati ŵayitutuzga galimoto, mbwenu galimto yila nyelemu/nyelemu-nyelemu mpaka mu dambo."

"A sambizi ŵakanipa chilango chakuti nikolele maji mu mawoko – kweni nyengo yose mbwenu maji nyelemu."

Nyenyenkhane[2]

This is from the verb "kunyenyenkhana" to tickle or fondle each other.

'nyenyenkhane' is in reference to a single act of tickling or fondling each other. If repeated, *'nyenyenkhane-nyenyenkhane'* is in reference to prolonged acts of caressing or tickling each other or one another.

"Mumalo mwakuti ŵakhale mwakukhazikika, mbwenu ŵana ŵala mu nkhwapa nyenyenkhane/nyenyenkhane-nyenyenkhane nakwamba kuseka."

Nyenyenkhe[2]

This is from the verb "kunyenyenkha" to tickle, or to caress or to fondle.

'nyenyenkhe' is in reference to the act of tickling or caressing. If repeated, *'nyenyenkhe-nyenyenkhe'* is in reference to prolonged acts of tickling or fondling.

"Mkakeni na Temwa pambele ŵandambe kusenga lukama, mbwenu ng'ombe yawo nyenyenkhe/nyenyenkhe-nyenyenkhe kuti yileke kujuta."

Nyete[2]

This is from the verb "kunyeteska" either to wet, or make wet, or to widen in coverage.

'nyete' is in reference either to the appearance of wetness or moisture, or a scenario of wide coverage – as with water in the lake, or – as with terrain in a wide

valley. If repeated, *'nyete-nyete'* is in reference to a much larger margin of the spread of water. Euphemistically, *'nyete'* has also been used in reference to one's body build being wide.

"Chigomezgo wati watunda, mbwenu kabudula nyete."

"Vula yati yawa, maji ghakachita kuti nyete/nyete-nyete mu dambo."

"Nyuma ya musungwana wane yikuchita kuti nyete."

Nyogodo

This is derived from the verb "kunyogodoka" to wilt.

'nyogodo' is in reference to being wilted – as with a crop that is dry and limp because of either heat or loss of moisture in the soil.

"Chifukwa cha chilala, mumela wose wachita kuti nyogodo mu minda."

Nyogodole[2]

This is from the verb "kunyogodola" to treat with ridicule, or to taunt.

'nyogodole' is in reference to the single act of taunting. If repeated, *'nyogodole-nyogodole'* is in reference to acts of taunting close to torturing.

"Mumalo mwakuti Tamandenji wamulumbe munyake, mbwenu iye nyogodole/nyogodole-nyogodole."

Nyomi

'nyomi' is in reference to large numbers of people or creatures surging into some single space – as with locusts into a garden.

"Ŵanthu ŵakachita kuti nyomi pa Boma ŵati ŵapulika kuti Mulongozgi wakwiza."

Nyongolore[2]

This is derived from the verb "kunyongolora" to twist out of shape.

'nyongolore' is in reference to the single act of twisting. If repeated, *'nyongolore-nyongolore'* is in reference to several acts of twisting so as to distort.

"Chifukwa cha nkhaza, mbwenu Fiskani chisulo chamunyake Dango nyongolore/nyongolore-nyongolore."

Nyong'onyong'o (also see "nong'onong'o")

This is from the verb "kunyong'omera" to being sweet.

'nyong'onyong'o' is in reference to the sensation of sweetness – as in sugar or candy.

"Chindongwa ichi chaphikika makola – chikuchita kuti nyong'onyong'o."

Nyongoroke[2]

This is from the verb "kunyongoroka" to be bent or twisted.

'nyongoroke' is in reference to the state of being bent or twisted. If repeated, *'nyongoroke-nyongoroke'* is in reference to the appearance of either many twists in an object, or the appearance of distortion in an object.

"Chifukwa cha kocha kwa moto, mbwenu chisulo chila nyongoroke/nyongoroke-nyongoroke."

Nyongoroske[2]

This is from the verb "kunyongoroska" to distort, or to twist, or to set at an angle.

'nyongoroske' is the act of bending, or twisting, or distorting. If repeated, *'nyongoroske-nyongoroske'* is in reference to repeated acts of bending and distorting an object.

"Chisulo chati chachesama pa moto, mbwenu Wanangwa chisulo chila nyongoroske /nyongoroske-nyongoroske."

Mumalo mwakuti mizele wanyoroske, iye mbwenu nyongoroske/nyongoroske-nyongoroske."

Nyoroske[2]

This is from the verb "kunyoroska" to make straight – as with a bent rod, or to correct – as with behaviour.

'nyoroske' is in reference to the act of straightening – as in a bent rod, or correcting, or counselling – as with behaviour.

"Wati watola chisulo chakugombeleka chila, iye mbwenu nyoroske/nyoroske-nyoroske."

"Nanga uli mwana wakaŵa wa mphuvya, nyengo yichoko waka mbwenu mukulu wake mwana yula nyoroske/nyoroske-nyoroske."

N'yoto

This is from the verb "kun'yotola" to stare blankly with wide open eyes.

'n'yoto' is in reference to that blank stare into open space.

"Tati tafika mu chipatala, tikasanga mulwali maso ghachita kuti n'yoto."

Nyukutu-nyukutu

This is from the verb "kunyukutula" to soften something such as a piece of paper, or bark, or to wash a piece of cloth briskly.

'nyukutu-nyukutu' is in reference to the feel of softness in something being washed such as a piece of fabric, or being modified as a piece of bark.

"Sopo yati yakwana makola mu malaya, kuchapa nako kukawa kwa nyukutu-nyukutu."

"Chifukwa cha kuwomba makola, chikwa chikachitanga kuti nyukutu-nyukutu apo tikapanganga nyanda."

Nyung'umizgu

This is from the verb "kunyung'umizga" to swallow the last dredges of something nice or delicious.

'nyung'umizgu' is in reference to the act of the tongue turning in the mouth with ecstasy and then swallowing.

"Fumbamtima wati wapakula wuchi na kunthonyezga mu mulomo, mbwenu wuchi wula nyung'umizgu."

Nyung'umu

This comes from the verb "kunyung'umuka" to move out, or leave discreetly.

'nyung'umu' refers to the act of leaving discreetely – as in leaving a place without being noticed

"Pala mwawona namunyinu nyung'umu, kuzizwa chala."

"Uko tichali pakati pa nchezgo, mbwenu Zizwani nyung'umu."

Nyung'unye[2]

This is from the verb "kunyung'unya" to suck something like a sweet in the mouth.

'nyung'unye' is in reference to the act of rolling and sucking that something in the mouth. If repeated, *'nyung'unye-nyung'unye'* is in reference to a done deal: rolled around and disolved.

"Mwiza wati wapokela switi, mbwenu switi yila nyung'unye."

"Awonani Chimango – mbwenu switi zaŵene zose nyung'unye-nyung'unye."

Nyutu²

This is from the verb "kunyutuka" to writhe – as in convulsions, or as when dying.

'nyutu' is in reference to a single movement of writhing. If repeated, *'nyutu-nyutu'* is in reference to acts of prolonged convulsions.

"Uko tikumupempherrela, mbwenu mwana yula nyutu/nyutu-nyutu."

Paŵa

This comes from the verb "kupaŵala" to lie relaxedly on one's back.

'paŵa' is in reference to the act of lying facing upwards.

"Zizwani wachita kuti paŵa pa msana wa ng'ombe."

Paghamu

This is from the verb "kupaghamuka" to fall suddenly from some height – as from a tree, or from a roof top.

'paghamu' is with reference to the motion of dropping without control.

"Fiskani wati wakwela mu khuni, mbwenu nakalinga paghamu wati wawona njoka."

Pangandale (see also "bagadale")

This is from the verb "kupangandala" to be out of line – as with teeth jutting the wrong way.

'pangandale' is in reference to the state of teeth being disorderly.

"Awonani Penjani – mino pangandale ngeti ngakufwindamo!"

Papaske²

This is from the verb "kupapaska" to move one's fingers softly over the surface of a body, or to explore a surface using one's fingers or palm.

'papaske' is in reference to a single stroke of touch over a surface. If repeated, *'papaske-papaske'* is in reference to several smooth palm or finger movements over a surface.

"Chidongo wati wawona kuti Lusungu wagona, mbwenu mu chiuno papaske."

"Chifipa wati wawona kuti kuli yiii, mbwenu mu mathumba ghamunyake papaske-papaske kupenja ndalama."

Paranthu[2]

This is from the verb "kuparantha" or "kuparanthuka" to writhe – as with a chicken whose head has been cut off.

'paranthu' is in reference to a single writhe. If repeated, *'paranthu-paranthu'* is in reference to continuous writhing.

"Apo tikasekeleranga kuti mwana wachila, mbwenu tasanga mwana paranthu/paranthu-paranthu."

Pataule[2]

This is derived from the verb "kupataula" to explain, or to make clear.

'pataule' is in reference to the act of explaining once or if repeated, *'pataule-pataule'* is in reference to the act of explaining in full.

Tinkhanani wati wafumbika kuti naye wayowoyepo, mbwenu iye vyose ivyo vikachitika pataule/pataule-pataule."

Patuke[2]

This is from the verb "kupatuka" to defecate, or to veer, or move out of the mainstream.

'patuke' is is in reference to either the act of defecating, or veering, or moving out of the mainstream. If repeated, *'patuke-patuke'* can be in reference to several acts of defecating, or veering, or acts of multitudes moving out of the mainstream.

"Uko mwana wakuwonkha, mbwenu mwana yula patuke."

"Uchizi wati wawona kuti kunthazi kukwiza madoda, mbwenu nthowa yila patuke kuti wabisame ku thondo."

"Chipani chati chamba waka, mbwenu ŵanthu patuke-patuke."

Patule²

This is from the verb "kupatula" to separate, or to divide into portions.

'*patule*' is in referene to the act of separating, or apportioning. If repeated, '*patule-patule*' is in reference to acts of separating objects.

"Dunduzu wati wapokela ndalama yake, mbwenu ndalama yila pakati patule kuti wamupeko mudumbu wake."

"Malizgani wati wafwatula thumba lake la kawunjika, mbwenu twakuvwala tula patule-patule."

Patuske

This is derived from the verb "kupatuska" to divert something from something else – as with a road.

'*patuske*' is in reference to the act of diverting.

"Tati tafika pafupi na mulonga, mbwenu musewu wula tikalimanga patuske kuti unyake ulambalale na dambo.

Pawu

This is from the verb "kupawula" to bring down – as with a fruit from a tree.

'*pawu*' is in reference to the bringing down of an object from a specific position – as with a fruit in a tree, or a hat from a hat holder.

"Tinkha wati waduka,,mbwenu chipewa cha ŵawiske pawu pa chimati."

Pengezu

This is from the verb "kupengezula" or "kupengezuka" to open one's nostrils widely, or to have one's nostrils opened widely.

'*pengezu*' is in reference to a state where nostrils are wide open.

"Chikhoso chati chamupweteka Chizaso, mphuno zikachita kuti pengezu."

Penthya² (also see "zenda")

This is from the verb "kupenthyama" to walk without balance – as with a drunken person.

'penthya' is in reference to the act of a single faltering step – as when walking. If repeated, *'pentyapentya'* is in reference to faltering movements or faltering steps – as one drugged, or hit and about to fall.

"Chiza wati wakhuta kachaso, mbwenu pakwenda penthya/penthyapenthya."

Pepetu²

This is from the verb "kupepetuka" to dry up – as with lips.

'pepetu' is in reference to lips showing signs of drying. If repeated, *'pepetu-pepetu'* is in reference to either a more serious indication of lips drying, or many lips showing signs of thirst.

"Chifukwa cha njala, mbwenu Sachizgo milomo pepetu."

"Madoda milomo yachita kuti pepetu-pepetu chifukwa cha nyota."

Pepu²

This is from the verb "kupepuka" to be light, or to be without weight.

'pepu' is in reference to being light. If repeated, *'pepu-pepu'* is in reference to being feather weight.

"Chifukwa chakuleka kulya makola, mwana wakuchita kuti pepu mu mawoko."

"Kankhuku ako ŵandipa kali pepu-pepu."

Pesu

This is from the verb "kupesuka" or "kupesula" to stoop and expose buttocks.

'pesu' is in reference to the act of stooping and exposing buttocks.

"Kamwana aka kalije nkhalo – awonani kachita kuti pesu pakati pa muzinda."

Petewu

This is from the verb "kupetewuka" to turn, or to change direction.

'petewu' is in reference to the act of turning around, or changing direction.

"Apo Mzondi wakakhumbanga kuyowoya unenesko, mbwenu petewu chifukwa cha wofi."

"Mathangeni wati wawona kuti ku thondo nkhwakukhola, mbwenu petewu."

Phaje²

This is from the verb "kuphaja" to roughly slice off – as with a bark of a tree, or with a carving.

'phaje' is in reference to the act of slicing off a piece once. If repeated, *'phaje-phaje'* is in reference to continued acts of removing pieces without symmetry.

"Thabwa liweme waka, mbwenu Chimwemwe thabwa lila phaje/phaje-phaje."

Phajule²

This is derived from the verb "kuphajula" to break off something from the main – as with a branch from a tree or a stalk.

'phajule' is in reference to a single act of breaking off a branch. If repeated, *'phajule-phajule'* is in reference to several such acts.

"Chimango wati wanjila mu munda, bwenu tuvivwati tose phajule/phajule-phajule."

Phakule²/Phakulule²

These are from the verbs "kuphakula" or "kuphakulula" to dish out from a cooking pot – as with sima.

'phakule' or *'phakulule'* is in reference to the act of a single dish out. If repeated, *'phakule-phakule'* or *'phakulule-phakulule'* is in reference to dishing out every morsel.

"Sima yati yapya, mbwenu Tapona sima yake phakule/phakulule or phakule-phakule/phakulule--phakulule."

Phalazge²

This is from the verb "kuphalazga" to announce, or to preach, or to spread word around.

'phalazge" is in reference to the single act of announcing or preaching – whereas if repeated, *'phalazge-phalazge'* is in reference to acts of repeated preaching or repeated announcements so as to leave no-one in doubt.

"Jika wati wapokela uthenga wa yifwa, mbwenu pa kaya pala phalazge."

"Muteŵeti wati wamala kuŵazga zivangeli, mbwenu phalazge/phalazge-phalazge."

"Nanga uli tikamukanizga Pachalo, mbwenu iye makani phalazge-phalazge."

Phange²

This is from the verb "kuphanga" to snatch – as with food or land etc.

'phange' is in reference to the act of snatching. If repeated, *'phange-phange'* is in reference to snatching everything – as with food, or with a shared cover.

"Nanga uli a fumu ŵakagaba makola malo, mbwenu Chiza malo ghaŵanyake phange/phange-phange."

Phapatizge² or Phapatizgu

These are from the verb "kuphapatizga" to squeeze through a narrow space.

'phapatizge' or *'phapatizgu'* are in reference to the act of slotting into narrow space. If repeated, *'phapatizge-phapatizge'* is in reference to repeated acts of squeezing into narrow spaces.

"Ziwone wati wawona kuti malo ghakukhala ghamala, mbwenu pakati pa ŵanyake phapatizge/phapatizgu."

"Wati wathila mafuta mu botolo, mbwenu chigamu phapatizge-phapatizge ku mulomo wa botolo kopa kuti mafuta ghangatayika."

Phayi²

This comes from the verb "kuphayila" to flap – as in an up and down movement of an eyelid.

'phayi' is in reference to the single flap of the eyelid. If repeated, *'phayi-phayi'* is in reference to several flaps of the eyelid.

"Mphepo yati yamuputa Lusungu, mbwenu maso phayi."

"Apo Mzondwase wakatenge wambe kulila, tikawonela maso kuti phayi-phayi."

Phirivu

This is from the verb "kuphirivuka" to suddenly change direction – as with a person or wind suddenly changing direction.

'phirivu' is in reference to that sudden change in drift, or in direction.

"Ngeti tifikenge pakaya, mbwenu Zizipizgani phirivu kuwelelaso ku nyanja."

"Apo tikatenge tose tili lumoza, mbwenu Nyamazawo phirivu."

Phuli

This is from the verbs "kuphulika" or "kuphuliska" to burst, or to burst open, or to let out.

'phuli' is in reference to the sudden burst – as with a tyre burst, or in reference to a sudden revelation – as with a secret being exposed.

"Chitufya chati chapya, mbwenu pachekha phuli."

"Nanga uli tikayezgeska kuti chikaya chileke kumanya, mbwenu makani ghala phuli."

Phuli²

This is from the verb "kuphulika" to glitter or to dazzle.

'phuli' is in reference to a single glitter of light – as in a siren lamp, or simply a single dazzle of brightness. If repeated, *'phuli-phuli'* can be in reference either to continued dashes of bright light, or sustained brightness – as in a well polished shoe or a clean shaven head.

"Nga kuti vula yambenge, mbwenu leza phuli."

"Mpala wa agogo ukuchita kuti phuli-phuli."

Phuluphutilu²

This is derived from the verb "kuphuluphutila" to fidget, or to be restless especially if in anticipation and being afraid of losing an opportunity.

'phuluphitilu' is in reference to a single act of restlessness – and if repeated *'phuluphitilu-phuluphutilu'* denotes continuous motions of being restless over an opportunity – as with a dog about to get some food.

"Sima ya nyama yati yafuka pa mphala, mbwenu ŵana phuluphutilu."

"Ncheŵe yati yanuska fungo la nyama, mbwenu phuluphutilu- phuluphutilu."

Phute²

This is from the verb "kuphuta" to blow – as into a fire, or to blow over a surface.

'phute' is in reference to a single act of blowing. If repeated, *'phute-phute'* is often in reference to the act of blowing off all dirt or dust from a surface.

"Fuvu lati lawa pa mpando, mbwenu Phelile fuvu lila phute/phute-phute."

Phuu

'phuu' is in reference to a waft of nice scent across one's nostrils.

"Mpunga wa ku Karonga uwu ukuchita kuti phuu pala waphya."

"Ndati ndajula botolo, mowa ukuchita kuti phuu."

Phwafu or Phwakatu

These are from the verbs "kuphwafula" to deflate, or "kuphwafuka" to be deflated, or "kuphwakatuka" also to be deflated, or to lose body.

'phwafu' is in reference to a state of being or having been deflated.

'phwakatu' is in reference to a state of losing or having lost body – as with a tube losing air, or a body losing weight.

"Bola lati lagwazika na munga, mbwenu phwafu."

"Soyaphi wati walwala sabata ziwili, mbwenu mwana thupi phwakatu."

"Mazaza wati wachomboleka, mbwenu matata phwafu."

Phwatu

This is from the verbs "kuphwatula" to forcibly tear along the seams or joints, or "kuphwatuka" to be torn along the seams.

'phwatu' is in reference to the sudden separation of the seams – as when once stitched together.

"Uko Zizwani wakuti waduke, mbwenu kabunthu phwatu."

Phwititi[2]

This is from the verb "kuphwititiska" to pierce through a piece of wood with a red-hot iron and in the process causing a gush of smoke.

'phwititi' is in reference to the outburst of smoke as a result of wood contact with the red-hot iron. It can also be in reference to a scene where there is a lot of dust raised in the air. It can also be in reference to a roudy atmosphere. If repeated, *'phwititi-phwititi'* is in reference to smoke, or dust rising everywhere, or in reference to the breaking out of chaos.

"Kavuluvulu wati wafika, mbwenu fuvu phwititi."

"Apo fikadololanga chaka, josi likuchita kuti phwititi."

"Nyumba yati yapya, mbwenu josi phwititi."

"Sunganani wati ukepo waka pa ungano wa chipani, mbwenu mbembe phwititi/phwititi-phwititi."

Phwitu

This is from the verb "kuphwitula" to forcibly break through skin, or surface with some tool.

'*phwitu*' is in reference to the sudden break in the skin, or surface as the instrument comes through.

"Apo Zeleza wakanjilanga pa thondo, mbwenu munga uli naye phwitu mukalundi."

Piku

This is derived from the verbs "kupikula" to lift, or to move towards an erection as a result of sexual excitement.

'*piku*' refers to the act of lifting, or the coming of rigidity in the male organ.

"Tati takhizga thumba mu galimoto. mbwenu Lazalo thumba lila piku nakunjila nalo munyumba."

"Mwana matuzi ghati ghamukola, mbwenu nthazi piku."

Pilili

This is from the verb "kupililika" to suddenly flow out at right angle to the surface – as in a broken water pipe, or the verb "kupililiska" to cause to flow out vertically.

'*pilili*' is in reference to that sudden vertical gush of fluid from a source.

"Timoti wati wagwaza ng'ombe na mukondo, mbwenu ndopa pilili."

Pilingizge

This is from the verb "kupilingizga" to cause an entanglement

'*pilingizge*' is in reference to the act of entanglement.

"Nyengo iyo Zondwayo wakati watimbe bola, mbwenu Tinkha wali naye pilingizge mu malundi."

Pilipiti² or Pilipitu²

This is from the verb "kupilipita" or "kupilipitila" to wriggle in pain, or because of restriction as with someone tied up.

'pilipiti' or *'pilipitu'* is in reference to the motion of wriggling. If repeated, *'pilipiti-pilipiti'* or *'pilipitu-pilipitu'* is in reference to continuous motions of wriggling.

"Kuti yende njoka ŵati ŵayitimba pa msana, mbwenu njoka pilipiti/pilipitu/pilipiti-pilipiti/pilipitu-pilipitu."

Pinkhu

This is from the verb "kupinkhula" to throw off something – as with a millipede, or a snail – using a stalk or some other tool.

'pinkhu' is in reference to the act of throwing off or tossing off an object with the use of a stalk.

"Bongololo wati wafika pafupi, mbwenu Palive wali naye pinkhu."

Pinthu²

This is from the verb "kupinthula" to throb or pulsate.

'pinthu' is in reference to a single throb. If repeated, *'pinthu-pinthu'* is is reference to continuous throbbing.

"Kawoko kati katupa, kakachitanga kuti pinthu/pinthu-pinthu."

Pipi

'pipi' is is in reference to the wafting of a foul smell or stench.

"Pa chimbuzi cha Soyaphi pakuchita kuti pipi."

Pipiku

This is from the the verb "kupipikuka" to be in erection.

'pipiku' is being rigid in the male organ.

"Nyuma wati wawona nthangalalo za musungwana, mbwenu nthazi pipiku."

Piringupiringu

This is from the verb 'kupiringuka" to be drifting in multitude and in all directions.

'piringupiringu' is in reference to that uncontrolled movement of people en masse.

"Pa yifwa ya Tata ŵanthu ŵakachita kuti piringupiringu."

Piriti[2]

'piriti' refers to the dipping of something into a hole. If repeated, 'piriti-piriti' refers to a prolonged plunge or entry into a hole.

"Njoka yati yapulika muswayo, mbwenu mu khululu piriti."

"Sato yati yachiluka, mbwenu mu buwu piriti-piriti."

Pizgu

This is from the verb "kupizgula" to turn something over at an angle, or "kupizguka" to be turned over, or to sprain.

'pizgu' is in reference to something turning over and left hanging at an angle, or spraining.

"Apo Zizwa wakati wayezge kunyamula mgololo, mbwenu mgololo wula pizgu."

"Wakati wanjila mukhululu mwasoka, mbwenu lundi pizgu."

Pokozo

This is from the verb "kupokozola" to remove a particle from something using a sharp instrument such as a tooth-pick or a finger.

'pokozo' is in reference to the act of picking or removing something – as from teeth, nose, or ear.

"Nyina wati wawona kuti mphuno za mwana nzakuzula, mbwenu mphonongo zila pokozo."

Ponoske

This is from the verb "kuponoska" to save, or to protect from danger.

'ponoske' is in reference to the act of saving or protecting.

"Ŵa sing'anga ŵati ŵamugwaza nyeleti, mbwenu mwana yula ponoske."

Porokoto

'porokoto' is in reference to hanging in abundance – as with fruits on a tree, or artefacts on someone's neck.

"Zalelapi wachita kuti mikanda porokoto mu singo."

"Matowo ghachita kuti porokoto mu khuni."

Poromu

This is from the verb "kuporomoka" to fall from a height – as from a roof-top

'*poromu*' is in reference to the sudden slide downwards from a height.

"Wati wakwela mukhuni, mbwenu Sunga poromu wati wawona njoka."

"Masanganavu ghati ghamukunga Zikani, mbwenu mukhuni poromu."

Porotu(o)

This is from the verb "kuporota" to go through – as in going through a forest, or through hurdles.

'*porotu*' is in reference to the act of getting onto the other side of the spectrum.

"Nanga uli moto ukakolela kose-kose, nyiska yikachimbila mpaka moto wula porotu(o)."

Pozomu

This is from the verb "kupozomoka" to let an object accidentally slip through one's hold.

'*pozomu*' is in reference to the accidental slipping of an object through one's grip.

Apo Vitumbiko wakati wathwike musuku wa maji, mbwenu msuku pozomu mu mawoko."

Pukulu

This is from the verb "kupukuluka" to be dumbfounded, or to lack the ability to respond.

'*pukulu*' is in reference to the act of not having the ability to react or respond to a situation.

"Wati wamanya kuti wakoleka, mbwenu Masozi pukulu."

"Ŵati ŵamugundika na mafumbo, mbwenu Phyoka pukulu."

Pulule[2]

This is derived from the verb "kupulula" to remove all leaves or fruit from a branch in a swoop.

'pulule' is in reference to the act of removing or clearing leaves or fruit from a branch in a swoop. If repeated, *'pulule-pulule'* is in reference to continued acts of clearing leaves from a stem or fruit from a branch until the branch is bare.

"Gomezgani wati wanjila mu munda, mbwenu yembe zose pulule/pulule-pulule."

Pundule² or Punduzge²

This is from the verb "kupundula" or "kupunduzga" to maim, or to cripple.

'pundule' or *'punduzge'* is in reference to a single act of crippling. If repeated, *'pundule-pundule'* or *'punduzge-punduzge'* refer to several acts of mutilating, or maiming.

"Musungwana wakutowa yula matekenya ghali naye pundule/punduzge/pundule-pundule/punduzge-punduzge."

"Soyaphi mbwenu muwoli wake punduzge-punduzge/pundule-pundule chifukwa cha kutimba."

Pupe²

This is from the verb "kupupa" to trim, or to spruce up – as with a lawn, or as with hair.

'pupe' is in reference to the one swoop of trimming. If repeated, *'pupe-pupe'* is in reference to trimming or mowing down every growth to base.

"Awiske ŵati ŵawona kuti sisi la mwana lakula, mbwenu sisi lila pupe."

"Chiyezgo wati wanjila mu munda mwa Fumbanani, mbwenu vingoma vyose pupe/pupe-pupe chifukwa cha kukwiya."

Purumu

This is from the verb "kupurumuka" to inadvertently lose ones grip over an object – as with an egg slipping through one's palms.

'purumu' is in reference to the slipping through of one's palms of an object by accident.

"Apo Lusungu wakapelekanga mphika wa dende kwa ŵanyina, mwasoka mbwenu mphika wula purumu."

Pute-pute

From the verb "kuputa" blowing – as of wind.

'pute-pute' is in reference to blowing.

"Wati wawona kuti pa mupando pali fuvu, mbwenu Mzamose fuvu lila pute-pute.

Putu-putu

This is from the verb "kuputuska" to cause to scatter objects through wind.

'putu-putu' is in reference to the flying of scattered objects because of wind – as with dust or dry leaves.

"Kavuluvulu wati wafika, mbwenu viswaswa putu-putu."

Puzu

This is from the verb "kupuzula" to deliberately deny one an opportunity, or deny one something that could be shared.

'puzu' is in reference to the act of depriving one of an opportunity.

"Sinya wali naye puzu Lazalo pakumulekela sima yambula dende."

Pwankhu

This is from the verb "kupwankhula" or "kupwankhuska" to leave widely open.

'pwankhu' is in reference to being totally open – as with a door left widely open, or a hole left without cover.

"Awonani mwa ŵana – munyumba mwachita kuti pwankhu!"

"Kumulomo pwankhu!"

Pyee

'pyee' is in reference to the act of scooping something from the ground.

"Tati tadekha, mbwenu Mapesi mboholi zithu pyee."

Pyepyetu

This is from the verb "kupyepyetula" to lift off someone from their feet by striking them in the legs so as to lose balance.

'pyepyetu' is in reference to the act of striking and throwing off someone through lifting them off their feet.

"Apo Yesaya wakati wapeleke njomba, mbwenu Gomezgani wali naye pyepyetu."

Ripiti[2]

This is from the verb "kuripitika" – to flow into some empty space in overwhelming quantity, or en masse.

'ripiti' is in reference to a single movement of mass into some empty space – as in soil being shoved into an open grave. If repeated, *'ripiti-ripiti'* is in reference to continued movement of mass or bodies into a hole or abyss.

"Tati takhizga thupi mu dindi, mbwenu ŵazukulu dongo ripiti/ripiti-ripiti mu dindi mula."

Rwii

This is from the verb "kurwita" to appear to be at a loss, or unwell.

'rwii' is in reference to someone appearing lost and as if in deep thought, or unwell.

"Wati wapokela uthenga wa ulwali wa munung'una wake, mbwenu Ndagha rwii."

"Kasi mwana uyu wati waka rwii – mwati wali makola?"

Saghali[2]

This is from the verbs 'kusaghalika' –to lie down on one's back, or "kusaghaliska" to fell – as with trees.

'saghali' is in reference to the act of lying flat out. If repeated, *'saghali-saghali'* would be in reference to several objects, or people lying flat out – as in a field of battle, or trees that have been felled.

"Nkhondo yati yamala, ŵanthu nawo ŵakachita kuti saghali/saghali-saghali."

"Mu magadi gha Chiukepo, makani ghatcheta kuti saghali."##

Sakaze[2]

This comes from the verb "kusakaza" to waste – as with resources, or to maim, or to mutilate.

'sakaze' is in reference to the act of wasting, or destroyimg, or mutilating. If repeated, *'sakaze-sakaze'* is in reference to the act of wasting everything, or destroying everything.

"Katundu yose uyo wakakhalako, mbwenu Chizaso sakaze/sakaze-sakaze."

"Masida galimoto yiweme yila mbwenu sakaze/sakaze-sakaze chifukwa cha zingozi zambula kumala."

Sakazike²

This is also from the verb 'kusakazika" to be wasted.

'sakazike' is in reference to a done deal – wasted. If repeated, *'sakazike-sakazike'* is in reference to total waste, or destruction.

"Chifukwa cha ulwali nyengo yitali, Tapona mbwenu sakazike/sakazike-sakazike."

Salanthu² (also see "paranthu²").

This comes from the verb "kusalanthuka" to twitch spasmodically – as when dying.

'salanthu' is with reference to a single twitch, whereas *'salanthu-salanthu'* is in reference to repeated or contionous twitches.

"Vinjelu wati watimbika nakuwa pasi, mbwenu salanthu/salanthu-salanthu."

Sambizge²

This is from the verb "kusambizga" to teach, or to counsell.

'sambizge' is in reference to the act of teaching, or counselling. If repeated, *'sambizge-sambizge'* is in reference either to a continous series of teaching, or completed series of teaching or counselling.

"Wati wanjila pa chiziŵa, mbwenu mwana yula sambizge/sambizge-sambizge kusyamba."

"Womama ŵati ŵawona kuti mwana wananga, mbwenu mwana yula sambizge/sambizge-sambizge mwakuti waleke kuwelezgaso."

Seŵere²

This is from the verb "kuseŵera" to play – as in a game, or recreation, or acting.

'seŵere' is in reference to a single round of playing or acting. If repeated, *'seŵere-seŵere'* is in reference to several rounds of playing, or acting.

"Tati tafika pa sukulu, mbwenu bola lithu seŵere/seŵere-seŵere."

Seŵereske²

This is from the verb "kuseŵereska" to play with some object, or to play a fooling game with a person with the other not realizing so.

'seŵereske' is in reference to the act of playing with something or someone. If repeated, 'seŵereske-seŵereske' is in reference to repeated acts of playing with something, or teasing.

"Chandiwira wati wawukapo, mbwenu Lazalo njinga ya Chandiwira yila seŵereske/ seŵereske-seŵereske."

Seke

This comes from the verb 'kuseka' – to laugh.

'seke' is in reference to the breaking into laughter.

"Ŵati ŵamuchilikita, mwenu mwana yula seke."

Sendame[2]

This is from the verb 'kusendama" to be at a tilt.

'sendame' is in reference to being tilted.

"Chindindindi ndi chati chamala, mbwenu nyumba nazo sendame/sendame-sendame."

Sendemu[2]

This is from the verb "kusendemuka" to move from an upright position to a slant.

'sendemu' is in reference to an object or objects moving from an upright position to a slanting position or positions.

"Uko chindindindi chili mukati, mbwenu nyumba nazo sendemu/sendemu-sendemu."

Sengenu (also see "songonu")

This is derived from the the verb "kusengenula" to melt by heating – as with ice into water, or fat into oil or from the verb "kusengenuka" to be melted.

'sengenu' is in reference to the turning of a solid into fluid, or the turning of a controlled situation to become worse.

"Moto wati wafikapo, mbwenu mafuta nagho sengenu mu poto."

"Chatonda wati wachilekela chilonda, mbwenu chilonda sengenu."

Sepetu or Sepetuke[2]

This comes from the verb "kusepetula" to hang down one's lips, or "kusepetuka" to have lips hanging down.

'sepetu' is in reference to lips or edges hanging down – as with a person, or dog, or as with a container.

"Apo Yezgani wakalilanga, milomo nayo yikachita kuti sepetu."

'sepetuke' is in reference to lips hanging down and out of shape. If repeated, *'sepetuke-sepetuke'* is in reference to total distortion of lips.

"Ulanda wati wamba kukwinyimbuka, mbwenu milomo nayo sepetuke."

"Uko wakulila Penjani, milomo nayo mbwenu sepetuke-sepetuke."

Sindame – (also see "sindi")

This comes from the verb "kusindama" to lower one's head – as a sign of respect, or dejection.

'sindame' is in reference to the act of dropping one's face

"Wati wawona a wiske vyala, Nyokase mbwenu sindame."

"Wati wawona kuti vinthu vikumuyendera chala, mbwenu Chimwemwe sindame."

Sindi[2]

This is also derived from the verb "kusindama" – to lower one's head down – as in grief.

'sindi' is the act of bowing one's head – as in sorrow, or dismay, or in respect. If repeated, *'sindi-sindi'* will usually be referring to a multitude – all with their heads down for whatever reason.

"Mzinda wose ukati waka sindi/sindi-sindi apo nyifwa yikafikanga."

Sindire[2]

This comes from the verb "kusindira" to compress or to pack closely – as with clothes into a suitcase, or as with loose soil into a hole, or over a surface, or as in closing a dead person's eyes.

'sindire' is in reference to a single act of pressing down over a loose surface, or in reference to closing eyes of a dead person. If repeated, *'sindire-sindire'* is in reference to several acts of compressing.

"Dongo lati layamba kuzula mu dindi, mbwenu dongo lila sindire/sindire-sindire."

"Chidongo wati wamalizgika, mbwenu maso sindire."

Sinizge

This is derived from the verb "kusinizga" to warn someone of something through a pinch, or a prod, or a flap of the corner of one's eye.

'sinizge' is thus in reference to the pinching or the flexing of one's eyelid to communicate a message or warning.

"Zikani wati wawona kuti nkhukhumba kuseka apo tikapulikizganga mulandu, mbwenu wali nane sinizge."

Sisite² or Sisitu²

This is from the verb "kusisita" to rub, or to caress, or to erase.

'sisite' is in reference to a single rub or rub out whereas *"sisite-sisite"or "sisitu-sisitu"* is in reference to a continous act of rubbing, or caressing.

"Ŵati ŵamba kuchezga, mbwenu Lazalo sisite/sisitu musana wa Maria."

"Wati wawona kuti wanangiska malemba, mbwenu malembo ghala sisite/sisite-sisite."

"Gomezgani wati wawona kuti Tafwakose wakumwemwetela, mbwenu musana wa Tafwakose wali nawo sisitu-sisitu."

Sizimile

This is from the verb "kusizimila" to close one's eyes.

'sizimile' is the act of closing one's eyes.

Apo ŵaliska ŵakati Tisope, mbwenu ŵanthu ŵose sizimile."

Sketu²

This comes from the verb "kusketula" to walk with feet dragging against the ground or floor.

'sketu' is in reference to the hiss as the foot drags against the floor. If repeated, 'sketu-sketu' is in reference to the continuous noisy sound of feet dragging along the floor.

"Kasi ninjani uyo wakuti sketu ku chipinda?"

"Mathangeni pakwenda ni sketu-sketu – kwali malundi ngazito!"

Skuke²

This is from the verb "kuskuka" to want to remain in a comfort zone.

'skuke' is in reference to the indication that you are comfortable and do not wish to be disturbed. If repeated, *'skuke-skuke'* is in reference to behaviour that indicates total absorption in borrowed comfort at the expense of one's own poor environment.

"Tati tamubweleka malaya, mbwenu Lazalo skuke/skuke-skuke mpaka tikachita kulondako na kukamupoka."

"Ŵati ŵamupokelera makola, mbwenu Chatonda skuke/skuke-skuke mpaka na kuluwa kwawo. Lekani sana zina lake ni Skukeya!"

Sokole²

This is from the verb "kusokola" to rouse, or to provoke, or to goad into action, or to spur.

'sokole' is thus in reference to the action of goading or spurring. If repeated, *'sokole-sokole'* refers to continued spurring or inciting into motion or action.

"Nkhuku zati zabisama mu utheka, Mateyo wali nazo sokole/sokole-sokole."

Sokomo/Sokomu

This comes from the verb "kusokomola" to flush out of hiding – as with wild game, or bees from their hive.

'sokomo/sokomuu' is in reference to the act of poking or prodding to cause dispersal.

"Kwambula kumanya ulwani wake, mbwenu Chimwemwe njuchi zila sokomo!"

Solomu

This is from the verb "kusolomoka" to slide downwards.

'solomu' is in reference to the downward movement of an object.

"Apo Zizwani wakati wimilile, mbwenu buluku nalo solomu!"

Soloto/Solotu (also see "porotu")

This is from the verb "kusolota" to go through – as through a forest, or through problems.

'*soloto/solotu*' is in reference to emerging out of the obstacle (also see "*porotu*").

"Sokayawo wakakhomezga mpaka soloto (u) mu visuzgo vyake."

Sompho

This stems from the verb "kusomphola" to elope.

'*sompho*' refers to that act of a man literally veering off a woman to get married secretely.

"Apo Mwiza wakaghanaghananga kuti ŵakuchezga, mbwenu Mazaza wali nayo sompho!"

Sondomu

This is from the verb "kusondomoka" to roll downhill.

'*sondomu*' is in reference to that sudden roll downwards – as with an avalanche, or with a boulder rolling down.

"Apo tikakhilanga lupiri, mbwenu kunyuma kwithu malibwe nagho sondomu."

Songo

This comes from the verb "kusongola" to sharpen the end of a tool – as with a stake, or pencil.

'*songo*' is in reference to the pointed sharp end of an object.

"Phesulo lachita kuti songo."

"Awonani Mbachi mu galimoto – kawoko songo pa chijalo."

Sotopo/Sotopu

This is derived from the verb "kusotopola" to cause to run out of hiding.

'*sotopu*' refers to that sudden jump from hiding – as with an animal running out of hiding because of impending danger

"Nyiska yati ya chiluka, mbwenu sotopo/sotopu."

Suku²

This comes from the verb "kusukunya" to shake.

'suku' is in reference to a single shove, or shake. If repeated, *'suku-suku'* is in reference to a repeated shake of back and forth movements.

"Wati wawona masuku mu khuni, mbwenu Pachalo khuni lila suku/suku-suku."

Sukuluke

This is from the verb "kusukuluka" to lose lustre, or glory.

'sukuluke' is in reference to the turning from glory or lustre to being plain.

"Salu yati yachapika, mbwenu skuluke."

"Chifukwa chaulanda, mama yula sono wachita kuti sukuluke."

Suluke²

This is from the verb "kusuluka" to fade, or to lose luster.

'suluke' is in reference to the beginning of fading. If repeated, *'suluke-suluke'* is in reference to a done deal: faded completely.

"Makatani ghachita kuti suluke/suluke-suluke chifukwa cha muhanya."

Sululu-sululu

This comes from the verb "kusulula" to leak – as through a grass-thatched roof, or through a cover that has defects.

'sululu-sululu' is with reference to the oozing of fluid as it passes through a cover or thatch.

"Vula yati yamba waka, mbwenu nyumba sululu/sululu-sululu."

Sungunu

This comes from the verb "kusungunula" to make lighter in density – as in paint using thinners, or as in wax over fire, or from the verb "kusungunuka" to be melted.

'sungunu' is in reference to the melting of mass into liquid.

"Vula yati yamala, mbwenu matalala nagho sungunu."

Sungunule

This is also from the verb "kusungunula" to melt or to make lighter in density.

'sungunule' here is in reference to causing melting to take place.

"Khoti wati wapika muthovu, mbwenu muthovu wula sungunule na moto."

Sungunuske

This is from the verb "kusungunuska" also to cause to melt.

'sungunuske' is thus in reference to causing melting to take place.

"Mafuta ghati ghakhoma, mbwenu Ŵalyenge mafuta ghala sungunuske pambele wandambe kuphika dende."

Sutule² (also see "fwatule")

This comes from the verb "kusutula" to loosen a knot, or to set free.

'sutule' is in reference to the act of loosening, or freeing something. If repeated, *'sutule-sutule'* is in reference to loosening or freeing totally.

"Mbateta wati wafika pa kaya, mbwenu nyozi zila wakakakila nkhuni sutule/sutule-sutule."

"Tambala uyo ŵakamukaka, mbwenu Zondwayo tambala yula sutule."

Swanu

This is from the verb "kuswanula" to tear skin around fingernails, or from the verb "kuswanuka" to have skin around fingernails torn.

'swanu' is in reference to the peeling off of skin around fingernails.

"Nkhafukula dongo mpaka mu njoŵe swanu."

Swayu

This is derived from the verb "kuswayula" to cause a rustle – as when walking or passing through thick dry grass.

'swayu' is with reference to the rustle as the object is going through some thicket or across dry grass.

"Apo tikati tikhale pasi kuti tipumule, mbwenu kuthondo swayu."

Swee

'swee' is with reference to the act of downing a drink with joy – as when thirsty

"Jando wati wajula botolo lake la phele, mbwenu swee."

Sweswetu

This is from the verb "kuswesweta" to sip – as when sampling a drink.

'sweswetu' is in reference to the act of sipping

"Wati wapokela jomela, mbwenu sweswetu."

Swi or Switu

This is derived from the verb "kuswita" to gulp, or to eat greedily.

'swi' refers to the act of pushing food through one's mouth in lumps, or chunks.

"Wati wamenya sima, mbwenu thozi lose swi/switu."

Swinyu

This is from the verb "kuswinyula" to contract muscles of the anus.

'swinyu' is the act of contracting the anus.

"Chiskuli chati chamukola Lazalo, mbwenu swinyu."

Taŵilile[2]

This is from the verb "kutaŵilila" to entwine, or to twist around an object – as with a creeping plant.

'taŵilire' is in reference to the creeping of the vine around a plant or a tree. If repeated, *'taŵilire-taŵilire'* is in reference to serious entwining that is almost chocking a plant.

"Awonani khuni ilo – mlozi wachita kuti taŵilire/taŵilire-taŵilire."

Tafya

'tafya' is in reference to a condition of helplessness resulting from either a serious beating, or illness – and lying there lifeless.

"Tumbikani wakatimbika mpaka tafya."

Taghalale

This comes from the verb "kutaghalala" to stand with legs wide apart.

'taghalale' is with reference to the position of legs being wide apart. If repeated, *'taghalale-taghalale'* is usually in reference to more than one individual standing astride.

"Chigomezgo wakutemwa kuti pala wimilira, mbwenu taghalale."

"Awonani ŵa silikali ŵachita kuti taghalale-taghalale."

Taghawu[2]

This comes from the verb "kutaghawula" to open legs wide apart when walking.

'taghawu' is with reference to a single movement of opening legs apart as one walks. If repeated, *'taghawu-taghawu'* is in reference to walking and opening legs outwards.

"Chifukwa cha vilonda mu nthangalaro, Chananga pakwenda wakuchita kuti taghawu/taghawu-taghawu."

Takamu

This comes from the verb "kutakamula" to raise one's arm with the intent to strike.

'takamu' is with reference to the act of raising the arm.

"Uko Dango wakuti takamu kuti watimbe Malango, mbwenu ŵanthu ŵamukola."

Takasu[2]

This comes from the verb "kutakasuka" to show signs of movement, or life while in a restrictive environment – as when bed-ridden, or while wallowing in poverty.

'takasu' is in reference to a single movement of life in a body. If repeated, *'takasu-takasu'* is in reference to several attempts to move.

"Pati pajumpha sabata yimoza, ndipo tikamba kuwona Mzondi kuti takasu/takasu-takasu pa mphasa."

Take[2]

This is from the verb "kutaka" to attack, or to invade.

'take' is in reference to the single move of attack. If repeated, *'take-take'* is in reference to total surrounding of an object – as when ants surround a piece of food, or as when red ants cover an enemy.

"Apo Tasokwa wakendanga mumudima, nkhulande zili naye take/take-take."

Takilile²

This is from the verb "kutakilila" also to attack, or to engulf.

'takilile' is in reference to the act of closely surrounding an object. If repeated, *'takilile-takilile'* is in reference to a total surrounding of an object – as with red ants attacking an object.

"Uko nyiska yikuti yichimbile, mbwenu mphumphi zili nayo takilile/takilile-takilile."

Talulire²

This is from the verb "kutalulira" to exaggerate, or to extend beyond a limit.

'talulire' is in reference to the act of exaggerating, or the act of extending beyond the expected limit. If repeated, *'talulire-talulire'* is in reference to exagarating way beyond the norm.

"Mateyo mumalo mwakuti wayowoye unenesko, mbwenu talulire/talulire-talulire."

"Mumalo mwakuti walime apo ŵakamulongola, mbwenu iye talulire/talulire-talulire mwakuti watole nalo ghanandi."

Tandike²

This is from the verb "kutandika" to make a bed, or to spread a blanket or cover over a surface.

'tandike' is in reference to the act of making a bed, or spreading a cover over a bed or a sleeping mat. If repeated, *'tandike-tandike'* is in reference to acts of making certain that a bed or beds are done.

"Kwati kwafipa, mbwenu Tiwonge mphasa yake tandike."

"Wati wanjila ku chipinda, mbwenu pakugona pake tandike/tandike-tandike."

Tang'a² or Tanga

These come from the verb "kutangaza" to walk wtih legs apart as a result of pain, or discomfort in the inner side of thighs.

'*tang'a*' or '*tanga*' are with reference to that strained movement, or walk with legs well apart. If repeated, '*tang'atang'a*' or '*tangatanga*' are in reference to several such painful steps.

'Malizgani wakuchita kuti *tang'a/tanga/tang'atang'a/tangatanga*' pakwenda chifukwa cha chitufya munthangalalo."

Tangalale

This is from the verb "kutangalala" to stand with legs far apart.

'*tangalale*' is in reference to the position of legs being well apart.

"Wati wimilila, mbwenu malundi tangalale."

Tanile[2]

This is from the verb "kutanila" to disallow participation from others – as with refusal to share anything with anybody.

'*tanile*' is in reference to a single act of ensuring that no one else has access to that something. If repeated, '*tanile-tanile*' is in reference to total closure to whatever could have been shared.

"Mdaghanjala pa kaya mbwenu minda yose tanile/tanile-tanile."

Taratara

This is from the verb "kutaratara" to fail to perform even when there is desire.

'*taratara*' is in reference to the fruitless effort in a given activity – as in a small ant fruitlessly trying to lift a morsel of food four times its size, or a spayed dog wanting to mount a bitch.

"Mabuchi tikamuphalia kuti nchito yila njinonono – mwamuwona sono wali taratara."

Tayu-tayu

This is from the verb "kutayuka" to relax.

'*tayu*' or "*tayu-tayu*" are in reference to feeling, or feelings of the body relaxing – may be because of an injection of some warmth.

"Nkhati namwa ka bibida, mbwenu thupi tayu."

"Ndati ndakhala pa kamuhanya, mbwenu thupi tayutayu."

Tegherezge

This is from the verb "kutegherezga" to listen attentively.

'tegherezge' is in reference to the act of listening with absorption.

"Fumu yati yamba kuyowoya, mbwenu wumba wose nawo tegherezge."

Teke (also see "neghe")

This is from the verb "kuteka" or "kutegha" to draw from a source – as with water from a container.

'teke/teghe' is in reference to the act of taking from a source.

"Chimango wati wanjila mu nyumba, mbwenu maji ghake teke/teghe."

Tekenyu

This comes from the verbs "kutekenya" or "kutekenyula" to crush.

'tekenyu' is in reference to the crushing of something into some mash.

"Galimoto yikamukanda kalundi mpaka tekenyu."

Tekenyu²

This comes from the verbs "kutekenyula" or "kutekenyuka" to dance in style, or to dance expertly on one's feet.

"*tekenyu*" is reference to a single but attractive movement in a dance. If repeated, *'tekenyu-tekenyu'* is in reference to continuous exciting foot movements.

"Thumbiko pa kuvina wakuchita kuti tekenyu/tekenyu-tekenyu."

Teketeke

This is derived from the verb "kuteketa" to crush into tiny particles.

'teketeke' is in reference to an object being crushed systematically into particles – as with terrmites breaking down dry grass.

"Galimoto yati yendapo, mbwenu mphasa yose teketeke."

Telemu²

This comes from the verb "kutelemuka" to slip off, or to be slimy.

'telemu' refers to the act of sliding as a result of the ground being slippery, or the slippery movement of food – as with okra, or mushroom.

"Uko nkhukhila mu lupili, mbwenu na munthu telemu."

"Nkhowani pakulya yikachitanga kuti telemu/telemu-telemu mu mulomo."

Tembelele[2]

This is derived from the verb "kutemba" or "kutembelela" to wish one ill-luck.

'tembelele' refers to the pronouncement of ill-luck over someone. If repeated, *'tembelele-tembelele'* is in reference to multiple ill-luck pronouncements being made.

"NyaSambo wati wamanya kuti Soyaphi ndiye wiba katundu wake, mbwenu Soyaphi yula tembelele/tembelele-tembelele."

Tembenu

This is derived from the verbs "kutembenuka" – to make a U turn, or to disclaim a situation, or "kutembenuska" to turn over an object.

'tembenu' is in reference to the act of physically making a U turn in position, or turning against, or as in a flip over.

"Apo pakwamba tikakolelana, mbwenu nunyane tembenu wati wawona kuti makani ghamba kusuzga."

"Apo nkhati nimuthaske Soyaphi, mbwenu iye tembenu – khofi mwaine."

"Galimoto yati yakhweta uheni-uheni, mbwenu tembenu."

Temu

This is from the verb "kutemula" to break skin – as in a serious bruise.

'temu' is in reference to the breaking of the skin as a result of friction.

"Uchizi wakagulumula mwana mpaka musana temu."

Temutemu

This is from the verb "kutemuka" to look radiant, or to glow – as in a female face.

'temutemu' is in reference to the oozing of radiance and smoothness of the skin – especially that of a female.

"NyaSato madazi ghano watowa – wakuchita kuti temutemu pa chisko.

Tendelu

This comes from the verb "kutendeluka" to be dumbfounded, or speechless.

'tendelu' is in reference to that sheepish look on someone dumbfounded or confused and unable to make a decision one way or the other.

"Wati wamanya kuti wasangika, mbwenu Yohane tendelu."

Te-te-te

'te-te-te' is in reference to a source being empty, or being bare, or being clear.

"Cheruzgo wamala dende lose te-te-te mu mbale."

"Ku mitambo kwachita kuti te-te-te muhanya wuno."

Tewutewu

This is from the verb "kutewuka" to lack strength in the knees.

'tewutewu' refers to the inability of knees to hold or carry one's weight.

"Chifukwa cha kuleka kulya zuwa lose mayilo, makongono sono ghakuchita kuti tewutewu pala nimilira."

Tezemu

This is from the verb "kutezemuka" to slip through one's grip or hold – often in reference to something breakable.

'tezemu' is in reference to an object suddenly slipping through.

"Apo Sunduzwayo wakati wanipile botolo la maji, mbwenu botolo lila tezemu."

Thaze[2]

This is from the verb "kuthaza" to spread out – as with knees, or to extend over a large area – as with government or authority, or as with grass or weeds coverage on fertile soil.

'thaze' is in reference to the motion of spreading out. If repeated, *'thaze-thaze'* is in reference to the act of spreading all over.

"Fumbanani wati wasendelera ku moto pa mphala, mbwenu thaze."

"Nchunga zachita kuti thaze-thaze mu munda."

Thi

'thi' is in reference to a body falling to, or collapsing to the ground.

"Takondwa wakatutuzgika mpaka pasi thi."

Thibu

This is from the verb "kuthibula" to beat to powder, or to pound or from "kuthibuska" to make an object look commonplace.

'thibu' is in reference to the act of hitting something as if it were a bag of sand.

"Uko Nyovani wakuti wadumule musewu, galimoto yili naye thibu."

Thibuthibu

This comes from the verb "kuthibuska" to make a once descent place a common place; or euphemistically, to make a once beautiful girl a plain one.

'thibuthibu' is in reference to the barenness as a result of over-use.

"Kumunda kwa amama kwachita kuti thibuthibu chifukwa cha ng'ombe."

"Jenala wachita kuti thibuthibu chifukwa cha ukavu."

Thizimu

This is derived from the verb "kuthizimula" to hit with brutal force with intent to maim.

'thizimu' is in reference to that horrible thud caused by brutal hitting.

"Uko muwoli wake wali mukati mukulongosola umo vinthu vikendela, mbwenu Nkazamuleke wali naye thizimu."

Thongathonga

This is from the verb "kuthongathonga" to be nervous and restless.

'thongathonga' is in reference to acts of nervousness and restlessness.

"Dingiswayo wati wamanya kuti ŵa polisi ŵakumupenja mbwenu thongathonga apo wakhala."

Thu or Thunye

This is derived from the verb "kuthunya" to spit.

'thu' or *'thunye"* is in reference to the act of spitting.

"Wati wapulika kuŵaba kwa munkhwala, mbwenu munkhwala wula thu/thunye."

Thuvu

This is from the verb "kuthuvuska" to cause to be lofty, or to be at great height.

'thuvu' is in reference to going or getting into heights.

"Nkhazamuleke wakatimba bola mpaka thuvu."

Thwanu

This comes from the verb "kuthwanula" to open one's eyes wide, or euphemistically, to begin to see in perspective.

'thwanu' is in reference to eyes opening wide. Euphemistically, it can also refer to being suddenly wise.

"Dokiso pakulaŵiska wakuchita kuti maso thwanu ngati ni kazizi."

"Pakuti sono mwavimyantha, sono muli thwanu."

Thwathwamu or Thwathwabu

These come from the verb "kuthwathwamula" or "kuthwathwabula" to pierce and break skin with something sharp – as with a horn (when bulls are fighting), or as with a piece of sharp wood.

'thwathwamu' or *'thwathwabu'* is in reference to the sudden appearance of a line over skin as a result of being gored.

"Apo nkhanjilanga pa thondo, munga wa mukhaya uli nane thwathwamu/thwathwabu pachiŵegha."

Thyabu

This is derived from the verb "kuthyabula" or "kuthyabuska" to cause water or liquid to splash.

'thyabu' is in reference to that sudden splash.

"Apo Deliwe wakaŵikanga msuko pasi, mbwenu maji thyabu."

Thya or Thyapu

These are derived from the verb " kuthyapa" or "kuthyapula" to whip.

"thya" or *"thyapu"* is in reference to the stroke of the whip landing on a body.

"Boti wati watola liswazo, mbwenu Mangaliso thya/thyapu."

Thyaku

This is derived from the verb "kuthyakula" to refine thick porridge – as in the final stages of preparing "sima."

'thyaku' is in reference to the act of turning the wooden spoon round the thick porridge in order to make it smooth and firmed up.

"Yati yamba kukhoma, mbwenu Tawina sima yila thyaku."

Tikite[2]

This is from the verb "kutikita" to crush to powder, or to apply pressure and friction to some surface.

'tikite' is in reference to a single act of crushing or applying pressure and friction. If repeated, *'tikite-tikite'* is in reference to either continuous acts of crushing, or acts of applying pressure and friction.

"Mbachazwa wati wanyaska hona, mbwenu hona lila tikite/tikite-tikite mu kawoko."

"Wati wagula mankhwala gha musana, mbwenu musana wose tikite/tikite-tikite'

Timbinyu or Timbwisu

These come from the verbs "kutimbinyula" or "kutimbwinyula" or "kutimbwisula" to crush, or to burst open – as with a tick, or a toad, or an egg.

'timbinyu' or *'timbwinyu'* or *'timbwisu'* is in reference to the bursting of an object and some fluid splashing.

"Wonenji wati watonthola nkhufu, mbwenu wali nayo timbinyu/timbwinyu/timbwisu."

Tindike[2]

This is from the verb "kutindika" to puzzle or to confuse.

'tindike' is in reference to puzzling. If repeated, *'tindike-tindike'* is in reference to puzzling beyond one's understanding.

"Mumalo mwakuti walongosole mwakupulikikwa, mbwenu iye ŵanthu tindike/tindike-tindike."

Tindikike[2]

This is from the verb "kutindikika" to be puzzled or confused.

'tindikike' is the feeling of being confused. If repeated, 'tindikike-tindikike' is in reference to being totally puzzled.

"Wati wayamba kuchita masalamusi, mbwenu banthu tindikike/tindikike-tindikike."

"Chilingwa cha ziŵalo chati chiza, mbwenu sukulu yose tindikike/tindikie-tindikike."

Tinye/Tinyu

This comes from the verb "kutinya" to crush an object between finger nails – as in crushing lice, or crushing something with wheels – as in something being run-over, or to strangle.

'tinye' or 'tinyu' is the act of crushing, or strangling.

"Wati wayiwona nyinda, mbwenu nyinda yila tinye/tinyu."

"Nyengoyawo wati wawona kuti wababa chilima, mbwenu mwana yula tinye."

Tokatoka

This is from the verb "kutokatoka" to be busy, or to work relentlessly – like a bee.

'tokatoka' is in reference to being relentlessly engaged in an activity, or being very busy over something.

"Ŵalendo ŵati ŵafika, Khataza mbwenu tokatoka."

Tololo

This is derived from the verb "kutololoka" to protrude upwards, or "kutololoska" to over-fill – as in a plate of food; or as in a basket, or in a container of sorts.

'tololo' is thus in reference to the mountain of something, or to too much luggage on a truck, etc.

"Sima yachita kuti tololo mu mbale."

"Katundu wali tololo mu galimoto."

Tombozge[2]

This is from the verb "kutombozga" to torture, physically or mentally.

'tombozge' is in reference to the act of torturing. If repeated, *'tombozge-tombozge'* is in reference to repeated acts of torturing.

"Ŵati ŵamujalira mu gadi Khetase, mbwenu musungwana yula tombozge/tombozge-tombozge."

Tondole[2]

This is from the verb "kutondola" to detatch nuts from their roots.

'tondole' is the act of detatching the nut from its root. If repeated, *'tondole-tondole'* is in reference to a continuous process leading to all roots cleared of their nuts.

"Ulemu wati wajima skawa, mbwenu skawa zila tondole/tondole-tondole."

Tonthole[2]

This is from the verb "kutonthola" to pluck, or pick off fruit.

'tonthole' refers to the act of picking off. If repeated, *'tonthole-tonthole'* is in reference to continued acts of plucking.

"Ŵana ŵanipweteka – awonani matatani ghane ghose mbwenu tonthole/tonthole."

Tototo

'tototo' is in reference to rigidity in an animal's tail, or in the male sexual organ, or in an arrow sticking out of a body.

"Usange nkhuzi yakalipa, mchila ni tototo."

"Ncheto yachita kuti tototo pa musana wa nyiska."

Tuku

This comes from the verb "kutukula" to lift upwards – as in a roof over a granary, or to pulsate repeatedly – as in a blood vein.

'tuku' could be in reference to the upward shove of a granary roof, or to a mole pushing through a surface, or as in a pulse.

"Pambere wandakwele munkhokwe, Suzgo wakdankha kaŵale tuku."

"Mwana uyu ndopa zikuchita kuti tuku-tuku mumisempha."

Tukulu²

This is from the verb "kutukuluka" to stir either in sleep, or move one's body when in restriction.

'tukulu' is is in reference to the stir. If repeated, *'tukulu-tukulu'* is in reference to continued movements – as when one is comimg out of deep sleep, or trying to get out of restriction.

"Apo tikatenge Chiphwafu wafwa, mbwenu tasanga tukulu/tukulu-tukulu."

"Tinkha wati wakakika mawoko na malundi, mbwenu tukuklu-tukulu."

Tukumu²

This is derived from the verb "kutukumula" or "kutukumuska" to inflate, or 'kutukumuka"– to be inflated.

'tukumu' refers to the movement in expansion as a result of inflating. If repeated, however, *'tukumu-tukumu'* may refer to the continuous expandion as one inflates – or it can be with reference to on'es acts of showing off and moving about haughtily.

"Tati tamba kupopa, mbwenu bola tukumu."

"Manyi nchifukwa chakuti wakwera vilingwa, Zakeyo pakwenda wakuchita kuti tukumu-tukumu."

Tukutuku

This is from the verb "kutukutuska" to rub one's skin with intent of making it warm.

'tukutuku' is in reference to the burning sensation under one's skin when rubbed, or when reacting to a chemical application, or a burning sensation in the eye resulting from a sting or an infection or simply in reaction to the existence of some foreign body.

"Palive wati waniphaka mankhwala, mbwenu musana wane wose tukutuku."

Tumphu

This comes from the verb "kutumphula" or "kutumphuska" to raise above a surface.

'tumphu' is in reference to the sudden appearance of an object above surface – as with a dead body suddenly appearing above the water surface, or as in one swimming under water and suddenly rising above the water surface.

"Mwana yula wati wabila, mbwenu nakale tumphu."

Tundumu

This is from the verbs "kutundunula" or "kutundumuska" to enlarge through inflating.

'tundumu' refers to the coming in of expansion as the object begins to fill with air

"Tati tamba kupopa bola, mbwenu bola lila tundumu."

"Manyi Muzipasi walikulyachi – nthumbo yachita kuti tundumu!"

Tungunyu (also see "timbwinyu")

This is from the verb "kutungunyula" to burst open as with a blister, or something holding fluid using a sharp tool like a needle.

'tungunyu' is in reference to the act of piercing and bursting a blister, or something holding fluid.

"Nanga uli Zuwayumo pakwamba wakchitanga mantha, paumalilo wali nacho chitufya chila tungunyu."

Tunkhu

This comes from the verb "kutunkhula" to break trough a surface – as in a mushroom breaking through the soil surface, or as with the coming of the breasts in a teenager.

'tunkhu' is with reference to the push of a mushroom's head through the soil surface, or the beginning of having breasts.

"Vula yati yawa, mbwenu nkoweni nazo tunkhu#."

"Nyengoyawo tumabele twamba kuti tunkhu."

Tunu

This is from the verb "kutunula" or "kutunuska" to stoop and raise one's buttocks at the same time.

'tunu' is in reference to the act of stooping and raising one's buttocks, or one's behind.

"Mkhalabweka wakachita kuti matako tunu apo ŵakamulasang nyeleti."

Tu-tu-tu

'tu-tu-tu' is in reference to foaming – as in milk that has come to the boil.

"Apo ŵakathilanga moŵa muchipindi, ukachita kuti tu-tu-tu."

Tuwulu

This is from the verb "kutuwuluka" to be covered in dust, or to lose colour, or to fade – as in a piece of cloth – or as in the hue of one's skin. Euphemistically, as when poverty has taken its toll.

'tuwulu' is in reference to looking out of colour, or poorly, or sallow.

"Pakufika, ŵanthu ŵakachita kuti tuwulu chifukwa cha fuvu mumusewu."

"Danile mungamumanya sono yayi – wachita kuti tuwulu."

Twatwazu

This is from the verb "kutwatwazula" to scratch something with something sharp like fingernails or thorns.

'twatwazu' is in reference to the scratching leading to drawing some blood.

"Uko Levi wakuti wabisame, minga yili naye twatwazu."

Twenyu

This comes from the verb "kutwenyula" to throw someone forcibly to the ground.

'twenyu' is in reference to the brutal and ncontrolled landing to the ground.

"Mwana wali nayo pasi twenyu."

Twi

This is from the verb "kutwika" to prick.

'twi' is in reference to the act of pricking.

"Lazalo wati watola sindano, mbwenu wali nayo Soyaphi twi."

Tyali

'tyali' is with reference to the act of squirting, or forcing out a small amount of liquid from a source – as in a squirt of urine.

"Manyi mbulala, Chatonda sono pakutunda ni tyali."

Tyankhu²

This comes from the verb "kutyankhula" to eat or chew noisily – often without closing one's mouth.

'tyankhu' is in reference to the noisy grinding of food between teeth. If repeated, *'tyankhu – tyanku'* is in reference to continued noisy chewing.

"Lazalo pakulya wakuchita kutii tyankhu/tyankhu-tyankhu."

Tyankhu

'tyankhu' on the other hand is in reference to being speechless – as when presented with hard evidence and unable to refute – or as when unable to answer when quizzed.

"Alufandika wati wachomboleka, mbwenu tyankhu."

Va

'va' is in reference to the act of putting a morsel into one's mouth with glee – as also sung in the children's song of "sono tiwelenge..."

"Mkakeni sima menye waka, mbwenu va."

Vikite²

This is derived from the verb "kuvikita" to violently hold by the neck and swing the object to and fro until it breaks – as in a dog killing a rabbit.

'vikite' is in reference to a single swing of the neck. If repeated, *'vikite-vikite'* is in reference to a done deal: broken up and finished.

"Ncheŵe yati yakola kalulu, mbwenu vikite-vikite."

Vikite²

This comes from the verb "kuvikita" to destroy into small pieces or particles – as with a dry piece of grass.

'vikite' is in reference to that single act of destroying. If repeated, *'vikite-vikite'* is in reference to the complete disintegration of the object.

"Wati wamupoka m'bada, mbwenu Zondwayo m'bada ula vikite-vikite."

Vivike²

This is from the verb "kuvivika" to roll and soil an object.

'vivike' is in reference to the rolling of an object in dust. If repeated, *'vivike-vivike'* is in reference to repeated acts of soiling an object. Euphemistically, *'vivike-vivike'* has been used in reference to subduing someone in a serious sexual activity.

"Ncheŵe yati yakola kalulu, mbwenu mudongo vivike-vivike."

"Wati wamubwakilila mwana, mbwenu mwana vivike-vivike."

Vivilu[2]

This comes from the verb "kuvivila" to roll oneself over the ground or soil.

'vivilu' is in reference to the act of rolling over. If repeated, *'vivilu-vivilu'* is in reference to a continuous act of rolling oneself over and over.

"Wati wafika pafupi na a nkhosi, mbwenu Jika pasi vivilu/vivilu-vivilu."

Vulukutu (also see "hulukutu")

'vulukutu' like *'hulukutu'* is in reference to the act of falling helplessly to the ground.

"Tafwachi wawa vulukutu."

Vulumu

This comes from the verb "kuvulumuka" to slip down – as in an over-sized pair of stockings sliding down.

'vulumu' is in reference to that sliding or slipping down of something worn.

"Uko wakwenda, mbwenu Lazalo buluku vulumu."

Vumbate

This is from the verb "kuvumbata" to close one's palms.

'vumbate' is in reference to the act of closing palms.

"Ndati ndaleka kumuseweleska, mbwenu mwana kawoko kake kala vumbate."

Vumbatile

This is from the verb "kuvumbatila" to enclose something in one's palm.

'vumbatile' is in reference to the act of enclosing something in one's palms.

"Ndati ndamupa kanthuli kanyama, mbwenu mwana yula vumbatile."

Vumpha

This comes from the verb "kuvumphama" to collapse headlong.

'vumpha' is in reference to the act of suddenly dropping one's head as one collapses – as in someone with a sudden heart failure problem.

"Uko tikuchezga naye, mbwenu mulwali yula vumpha."

Vundike

This is derived from the verb "kuvundika" to roast a tuber under hot ash, or to cover wild fruit in warm soil so as to ripen it.

"vundike" is in reference to the act of thrusting a tuber or fruit into hot ash, or into warm earth.

"Wati wakhwema masuku ghakhe, mbwenu Pasipawo masuko ghala vundike mukhululu."

Vundu

This comes from the verb "kuvundula" to stir, or to arouse.

'vundu' is in reference to the act of stirring or arousing a situation.

"Wati watola muthiko, mbwenu mumowa mula vundu."

Vundule[2]

This is also from the verb "kuvundula" to stir, or to excite.

'vundule' is in reference to the act of stiring – as with moving a spoon around some liquid, or the act of exciting or stimulating something. If repeated, *'vundule-vundule'* is in reference to continued acts of stirring, or stirring up, or bringing out something conveniently forgotten.

"Songiso wati wafika pa chisime, mbwenu maji vundule/vundule-vundule."

"Apo tikatenge taluwako, mbwenu Vilije makani ghala vundule/vundule-vundule."

Vundumu

This also comes from the verb "kuvundumula" to disturb, or to upset.

'vundumu' is in reference to the sudden onrush of something because of being disturbed – as with a swarm of bees, or as in a sudden upset of one's stomach – as when there is too much acid.

"Gadi wati wamwa kachasu, mbwenu munthumbo vundumu."

"Apo Mzondi wakati njuchi zila vundumu, zose zikamalira mwa iye."

Vungulike

This is from the verb "kuvunguliska" to carve out, or to craft something with depth – as in a wooden fruit bowl or as in a wooden plate.

'vungulike' is in refrerence to a surface that is not flat – but something that is in the shape of a trough.

"Likhezo lachita uti vungulike."

Vungumale

This is from the verb "kuvungumala" to draw or curve one's shoulders inwards.

'vungumale' is in reference to shoulders curving inwards – as when one wants to display some self praise or self confidence.

"Mwamuwona Levi wachita kuti vungumale pakukhala."

Vupu

This is from the verb "kuvupula" to hit hard – usually using a stick.

'vupu' is in reference to the act of hitting hard. (*See "dyuku"*)

"Uko Chiukepo wakuti waponye nthonga, Tembani wali nayo vupu mumusana."

Vutupu (also see "vwatapu")

This comes from the verb "kuvutupula" or "kuvutupuska" – to chase out of hiding – as with prey in a forest or bush.

'vutupu' is in reference to that act of suddenly jumping out of bush – as with game

"Nyiska yati yanuska ulwani, mbwenu vutupu."

Vutuvutu

This is derived from the verb "kuvutuska" to make a place look over-used or thoroughly bare.

'vutuvutu' is in reference to a state of looking thoroughly bare, or plain because of over-use – as with mice tracks, or a playing field.

"Awonani pakhululu la mbewa pachita kuti vutu-vutu."

Vuu

'*vuu*' is in reference to a large crowd sitting quietely.

"Apo tikafikanga,tikasanga ŵanthu ŵali vuu pawalo."

Vuŵate

This is from the verb "kuvuwata" to leave stored in the mouth.

"*vuwate*" is in reference to that act of placing something in the mouth and leaving it stored there – as in deliberately not wanting to swallow what is in one's mouth.

"Mumalo mwakuti wamize mankhwala, mbwenu Lazalo mankhwaka ghala vuwate."

Vwamphu

This is from the verb "kuvwamphula" to let go – as with a trap.

'*vwamphu*' is in reference to the sudden release of a trap.

"Uko mjancha ukulya kausipa, mbwenu msampha vwamphu."

Vwatapu (also see "vutupu")

This is from the verb "kuvwatapuska" to bring out of hiding – as with game.

'*vwatapu*' is in reference to the sudden jump from hiding, or sleep – as with game that has sensed danger nearby.

"Kalulu wati wapulika kubwentha kwa ncheŵe, mbwenu vwatapu pa chivwati."

Vwavwalala

'*vwavwalala*' is in reference to the act of falling to the ground in a heap – or helplessly – or without resistance, or without energy – as in a bird falling to the ground because it has broken wings.

"Mzondi wakatimba Nyuma na nthonga mpaka Nyuma napasi vwavwalala."

Vwi

This is from the verb "kuvwita" to dip in some substance.

'*vwi*' is in reference to the act of dipping into substance – as into sand, soil, sugar, food – with intent to scoop.

"Khetase wati watola mbale, mbwenu mu ufu vwi."

Vwinkhu

This comes from the verb "kuvwinkhula" to jiggle vulgarly.

'vwinkhu' is in reference to that quick and short forward movement of one's waist or hip with vulgarity- as in a vicious sex act.

"Gomezgani pakuvina wakuchita kuti vwinkhu."

Vwiti

This is derived from the verb "kuvwitika" or "kuvwitizga" to pierce deeply – as with a spear into a body of an animal or person.

'vwiti' is in reference to the act of plunging – as with a spear or knife going through some body to the hilt.

"Mazaza wati watola mkondo, mbwenu mwa Muwuso vwiti."

Vwitike

These come from the verb "kuvwitika" to insert deeply – as a spear or arrow into an animal's body.

'vwitike' is in reference to the act of inserting deeply.

"Fiskani wati wajula chimayi, mbwenu musingo la Soyaphi vwitike."

Vwivwilili

'vwivwilili' is in refrerence to the act of falling helplessly to the ground – as in a knock-out, or as the result of a rough push.

"Fumbamtima ŵakamutimba mpaka mudongo vwivwilili."

Vwivwilizu

'vwivwilizu' is also in reference to the act of falling helplessly to the ground but with the face hitting the ground first.

"Nezala wakawa chakavunama mpaka mphuno mudongo vwivwilizu."

Vyali

This is derived from the verb "kuvyalika" to pass on an imaginary burden onto someone by touching them – and expected to pass it back, or to pass it on to another person (a children's game called "kavyali").

'vyali' is the act of quickly contacting the other person indicating that the burden has been passed on.

"Hlekiwe wati wadekha, mbwenu munyake wali naye vyali pa phewa."

Vyapu

This is derived from the verb "kuvyapula" to thrash to pulp – or to senselessness.

'vyapu' is in reference to that act of walloping, or hitting hard as in a thrash. In other areas the ideophone is *'vwapu'* from the verb "kuvwapula."

"Apo Sangulukani wakati wachimbile, Chananga wali naye vyapu na liswazo."

Vyongonyo or Vongonyo or Vyanganyu

These come from the verbs "kuvyongonyola" or "kuvongonyola" or "kuvyanganyula" to dislocate, or "kuvyongonyoka", or "kuvongonyoka" or "kuvyanganyuka" to be dislocated.

'vyongonyo' or *'vongonyo'* or *'vyanganyu'* are in reference to the dislocation having been completed.

"Songiso wati watimba bola lila, mbwenu khongono lake nalo vyongonyo/vyongonyo/vyanganyu."

Waa

This is from the adjective "kuwawa" painful (bodily pain), or bitter in taste, or sour.

'waa' is in reference to that wave of pain – as in body, or sourness or bitterness – as in food or a beverage.

"Ndati ndaphaka mankhwala pa nganga, mwenu ngaga yose waa."

"Mchele wachita kuti waa mu dende."

Waghawagha

'waghawagha' is in reference to being loose – as with to and fro movements of a door-frame that is not well fixed to the walls – or as with a bicycle wheel that is not tight.

Euphemistically, *'waghawagha'* has been used to apply to looseness of one's morals.

"Chijalo ichi chikakhomeka makola chara – awonani chilli waghawagha."

"Hlezipe nkhalo ni waghawagha."

Walawala

'*walawala*' is in reference to loss of direction, or loss of flow – as in an argument, or as in failing to find a solution to a problem.

"Tawonga wati wafumbika kuti walongosole makola, mbwenu walawala."

Wee

This is from the verb "kuweska" to insert, or to thrust into something.

'*wee*' is in reference to the act of inserting, or entering into something – as with a male organ into a female organ, or a knife into flesh.

"Chiyezgo wati wiba chimayi, mbwenu mu nchinda ya utheka wee."

Weteke

This is from the verb "kuweteka" to insert.

'*weteke*' is in reference to the act of inserting.

"Wati wasola chipula, mbwenu mu nchinda ye utheka weteke."

Wewelele

'*wewelele*' is in reference to entry into something shrouded, or protected, or concealed.

"Chiza kwambula nakuwodila chala, mbwenu munyuma yaŵene wewelele."

Wofuwofu

This is from the adjective "kuwofoka" to be soft – as with a cushion.

'*wofuwofu*' is in reference to the feel of softness – as in a cushion, a mattress, a sofa, a carpet, etc.

"Mipando yakwithu yikuchita kuti wofuwofu pala wakhalapo."

Woliwoli

'*woliwoli*' is in reference to a state of being over-ripe – as with an over-ripe fruit, or over-cooked meat.

"Nchunga zikapya mpaka woliwoli."

Wonju

This is from the verb "kuwonja" or "kuwonjola" to catch – as in fish with a hook, or to capture – as with a bird over a trap.

'wonju' is in reference to the act of capturing.

"Uko somba yikulyela, Fumbanani wali nayo wonju."

Wulawula

This is from the verb "kuwulawula" to move, or walk without direction – as with a blind person.

'wulawula' is in reference to walking about blindly, or without a sense of direction, or the act of failing to come up with a convincing argument.

"Umo maso ghali kudolokela, Nyengoyawo pakwenda sono ni wulawula."

"Songelwayo wati wafika pa mphala, mbwenu wulawula pakuyowoya."

Wuluwulu

'wuluwulu' is in reference to the beginning of swelling in a limb as a result of a sting, a burn or a whip.

"Njoka yati yamuluma Tifapi, mbwenu kalundi wuluwulu."

Wundumu

This is from the verbs "kuwundumula" to pull down – as with a wall, or "kuwundumuka" to disintegrate – also as with a wall.

'wundumu' is in reference to sliding down of mass – as in a broken wall, or as in a mud slide.

"Chiliŵa chati chanyewa, mbwenu wundumu."

Wunguzu

This comes from the verb "kuwunguzula" to rip or tear away a top skin – as in skin over a wound.

'wunguzu' is in reference to the ripping, or tearing away surface skin.

"Apo tikauskangapo bandeji pa chilonda, mbwenu chikumba chapachanya nacho wunguzu."

Wuwe

This is from the verb "kuwuwa" to lose luster, or to lose splendour, glory, or glow.

'wuwe' is in reference to the appearance of neglect – as in a ruin, or a person once radiant but now derelict.

"Pakaya pakwithu pachita kuti wuwe ngati palije ŵanthu."

"Malita wachita kuti wuwe-wuwe naumo walikuwelera ku nthengwa."

Yaghawu[2]

This is derived from the verb "kuyaghawula" to open one's inner thighs indecently – often in the case of women.

'yaghawu' is thus in reference to the act of opening one's thighs and without due care. If repeated, *'yaghawu-yaghawu'* is in reference to repeated acts of opening one's inner thighs.

"Musungwana yula nkhalo walije – apo wakhala mbwenu milezi yaghawu/yaghawu-yaghawu."

Yaghayagha

This comes from the verb "kuyaghayiska" to shake up, or to cause to shake up – as with the passing of an earthquake.

'yaghayagha' is in reference to the shaking of mass – as with a building because of an earthquake, or in a person simply out of fear, anxiety or being overwhelmed.

"Kwati kwafika chindindi, nyumba zose mbwenu yaghayagha."

Yaghayizge

This is from the verb "kuyaghayizga" to simulate, or to pretend – as with one's emotions.

'yaghayizge' is in reference to the act of simulating or pretending.

"Panyengo yakuti ŵamlenge ulendo wawo, mbwenu Deliwe ulwali yaghayizge kuti wakhale.

Yanda

This comes from the verb "kuyandama" to come from below the water surface and float lifelessly.

'yanda' is in reference to the lifeless floating of an object on the surface of water or liquid – as with a dead fish.

"Somba zati zafwa chifukwa chamunkhwala mumaji, mbwenu zose yanda."

Yangazu

'yangazu' is in reference to being dumbfounded, or being speechless, or being confused and lost.

"Chuma chati chamumalila Tasokwa, mbwenu yangazu."

Yanule[2]

This is from the verb "kuyanula" to remove garments from a clothes line, or to remove flour from a drying zone, or to remove a blanket or cover from a sleeping place.

'yanule' is the act of removing clothes from a line or a cover from a bed. If repeated, 'yanule-yanule' is in reference to repeated acts of removal.

"Wati wawuka mu tulo Soyaphi, mbwenu mphasa yake yanule."

"Siyenji wati wawona kuti kukwiza vula, mbwenu wufu wake yanule."

"Malaya ghati ghamila, mbwenu Maria malaya ghala yanule-yanule."

Yasa

This is from the verb "kuyasama" to open one's mouth widely.

"Wati wapulika kuti watondenga vilingwa, mbwenu Tafwachi kumulomo yasa!"

Yelekezge

This is derived from the verb "kuyelekezga" to compare, or to simulate.

'yelekezge' is in reference to the act of comparing, or simulating.

"Uko tikuseŵela, mbwenu Maria yifwa yelekezge."

"Wati wagula malaya ghake, mbwenu yelekezge na malaya gha Pasipawo."

Yende or Yendu

This is from the verb "kuyenda" or "kwenda" to walk.

'yende' or 'yendu' is in reference to the act of a single step – as in a toddler making an attempt to walk.

"Uko mwana tikuti da-da-da, mbwenu mwana yula tasanga yende/yendu."

Yenja (also see "yanda")

This is derived from the verb "kuyenjama" to float.

'yenja' is in reference to floating – as in a dead body floating – or a piece of wood floating.

"Ŵati ŵathilamo mankhwala mu Nyanja, somba zose mbwenu yenja."

Yepu

This is from the verb "kuyepula" to trim – as with hair.

'yepu' is in reference to a single act of trimming, or pruning into good shape.

"Mahlasi wati watola sizala, mbwenu sisi zamwana yepu."

Yeyelu-yeyelu

This comes from the verb "kuyeyela" to have itching teeth as a result of biting into something acidic – such as an unripe green mango, or some other sour fruit.

'yeyelu-yeyelu' is in reference to the itching of teeth.

"Ndati ndalya yembe yaŵisi, minu ghane ghakachita kuti yeyelu-yeyelu."

Yimilire

This is from the verbs "kuyimilila" or "kwimilila" to stand up.

'yimilile' is in reference to the act of standing up.

"Mwakawona kamunkhwele kachita kuti yimilile."

Yindu[2]

This is derived from the verb "kuyindula" to steam – as in cooking, or to stir up – as in instigation.

'yindu' is in reference to the single act of stirring, or stirring up. If repeated, *'yindu-yindu'* is in reference to the coming of stimulation in reaction to some stir – as with the coming on of a spread of rash over skin in reaction to some irritation.

"Ŵati ŵamumweska nkhama mwana, mbwenu nthomba yose yindu muthupi."

"Kaŵaŵa wati wanjila mumaji, mbwenu dongo lapasi yindu-yindu mumaji."

Yingisu-yingisu or Yingitu-yingitu

These are from the verb "kuyinga" to wander aimlessly, or move about without a definite destination or aim.

'yingisu-yingisu' or *'yingitu-yingitu'* is in reference to moving up and about aimlessly.

"Ŵanthu ŵakachita kuti yingisu-yingisu pa ungano wajuzi."

Yiriyiri

'yiriyiri' is in reference to the passing of tremors through one's skin, or body as a result of fear, or cold, or anger.

"Kamphepo kati kanikhwasa, thupi likachita kuti yiriyiri."

"Ndat ndapulika kuswaya kunyuma kwane, mbwenu thupi nalo yiriyiri."

Yo

'yo' is in reference to a container being full — as with grain in a basket.

"Ngoma zachita kuti yo muchidundu."

Yorokoto (see "porokoto")

'yorokoto' is in reference to being abundant — as with fruit in a tree, or trinkets around a neck.

"Mikanda yachita kuti yorokoto mu singo la Khetase."

Yoyotayoyota

This is from the verb "kuyoyotala" or "kuyoyotila" to move or walk with uneven steps as a result of loss of strength, or energy because of ill-health.

'yoyotayoyota' is in reference to the awkward and weak movements of something not well.

"Chifukwa chakulwala nyengo yitali, Boti pakwnda sono ni yoyotayoyota."

Yo-yo-yo

This comes from the verb "kuyoyoska" to cause to drop in plenty — as in fruits from a tree, or as in a drizzle, or tears.

'yo-yo-yo-yo' is in reference to the drop of fruits, rain, tears – or money in plentiful quantity.

"Kumbukani wakatimbika mpaka masozi yo-yo-yo."

"Thumba lati lapaluka, bwenu ndalama nazo yo-yo-yo."

Yungunu²

This is from the verb "Kuyungunula" to spin or to swirl, or turn with a whirling motion.

'yungunu' is in reference to the act of spinning or swirling – as in a woman spinning a skirt or dress. If repeated, *'yungunu-yungunu'* is in reference to repeated spins.

"Para Tapona wakwenda, malaya ni yungunu/yungunu-yungunu."

Yungwayungwa

This is from the verb "kuyungwa" to be left in the cold, or to be lonely and desperate, or in despair.

'yungwayungwa' is in reference to that restless behaviour as a result of being lonely and in despair.

"Ŵapapi ŵose ŵati ŵafwa, ŵana mbwenu yungwayungwa."

Yu-yu-yu (see "pepu")

This is from the verb "kuyuyuka" to be of light weight.

'yu-yu-yu' is in reference to the feel in the palms of something being very light in weight.

"Mwana uyu wakuchita kuti yu-yu-yu mu mawoko."

Zakazaka

'zakazaka' is in reference to a state of (i) inability to move one's limbs as a result of lack of energy (ii) inability to talk as a result of being overwhelmed, (iii) inability to perform, and (iv) inability to remain steady – as in a person trembling out of fear, or illness.

"Tifapi khumbo lakwenda wakaŵa nalo – kwene apo wakati wayezge mbwenu zakazaka."

"Songiso wakati wayezgele umu na umu kulongosola, mbwenu zakazaka."

Zare-zare

This is from the verb "kuzara" to be in plentiful supply as in commodities.

'zare-zare' is in reference to things, money, people – being in plentiful supply – everywhere.

"Vyakulya panyumba ya ŵa sekulu ni zare-zare."

Zelezeke[2]

This is from the verb "kuzelezeka" to become insane, or deranged, or out of one's mind.

'zelezeke' is in reference to the state of loss of one's orderliness – or the loss of one's sanity.

"Chifukwa chakukweŵa chamba nyengo na nyengo, mbwenu Sothini zelezeke."

"Wati wapulika kuti nyumba yake yapya yose, mbwenu Soyaphi zelezeke/zelezeke-zelezeke."

Zelezge

This is from the verb "kuzelezga" to ignore, or to disregard deliberately.

'zelezge' is the act of ignoring or intentionally disregarding something.

"Nanga uli Vinjelu ŵakamuphalila kuti waleke mbwenu iye dala zelezge."

Zemu

This stems from the verb "kuzema" to lightly touch a woman's breast – often without her permission.

'zemu' is in reference to the act of touching, or stroking lightly a woman's breast.

"Zalelapi wati wadekha, Mazaza wali naye zemu pabele."

Zenda[2]

This is from the verb "kuzendama" to walk unsteadly and without balance – as one who is drunk or drugged.

'zenda' is in reference to the act of walking unsteadly and without balance. If repeated, *'zenda-zenda'* is in reference to a continuous unsteady walk.

"Apo Chiwukepo wakafumanga mu chipatala, kwenda kukawa kwakuti zenda."

"Zeleza wati walowêla, mbwenu pakwenda zenda-zenda."

Zeteku²

This comes from the verb "kuzetekula" to gallop – as with a horse or a cow.

'*zeteku*' is in reference to the act of a single gallop. If repeated, '*zeteku-zeteku*' is in reference to galloping away.

"Mwamuwona Jenda-yekha, pakwenda wakuchita kuti zeteku/zeteku-zeteku."

Zeza

'*zeza*' is in reference to a state of being stunned, or dumbfounded – maybe with shock, or because one is suddenly confounded, or bewildered and speechless, or confused.

"Lati lakoleka kuti likwiba, mbwenu doda zeza."

"Mzondi wati wamanye kuti munyakhe ndiyo wakwenda na muwoli wake, mbwenu zeza."

Zezelu

This is derived from the verb "kuzezeluka" to have a rude awakening, or to suddenly come to reality – as being out of a dream.

'*zezelu*' is in reference to the act of sudden realization of circumstances or environment.

"Ŵati ŵamuthila maji ghakuzizima, mbwenu Tumbikani zezelu."

"Wati wamanya kuti mbunenesko, ndipo watenge zezelu."

Zge²

This is from the verb "kuzgeta" to quickly go past one's sight.

'*zge*' is in reference to a single and fast movement of an object past the eye. If repeated, '*zge-zge*' is in reference to fast movements of an object passing between two frames more than once.

"Tati takhala pa khonde, mbwenu kayuni zge."

"Tati takhala pa khonde, mbwenu tuyuni nato zge-zge."

Zgee or Zgelele

'zgee' or *'zgelele'* is in reference to either the fading of light – as when the sun has set, but darkness is yet to set, or when dawn is breaking but it is still difficult to see far.

"Pala zuwa lanjila, kuwalo nako kukwamba kuti zgee/zgelele."

"Apo fikawukanga, kukaŵa kuti kumatandakucha nako kuafi## zgee."

Zgetu²

This is derived from the verb "kuzgeta" to quickly go past the eye, or to quickly go past two frames.

'zgetu' is in reference to a single and fast movement of an object past the eye. If repeated, *'zgetu-zgetu'* is in reference to repeated movements of an object past the eye.

"Tati fike waka mu thengere, mbwenu kakalulu zgetu."

"Pambele vula yindawe, tikawonanga waka ŵakaŵeluŵelu zgetu-zgetu."

Zgoli²

This comes from the verb "kuzgolika" to bend the neck and consequently the head downward.

'zgoli' is in reference to the stooping of one's head – often because one is overwhelmed by grief, or shame, or shyness. If repeated, *'zgoli-zgoli'* is in reference to either continued acts of lowering one's head, or more than a single head that has been lowered.

"Ulemu ŵati ŵamuchenya, mbwenu mwona zgoli."

"Apo tikafikanga, tikasanga ŵanthu ŵali zgoli-zgoli."

Zgu

This stems from the verb "kuzgula" to uproot or to pull out by the roots.

'zgu' is in reference to the uprooting being completed.

"Fumbani na Lazalo bakalimbana nalo khuni mpaka zgu."

Zikitizge[2]

This is from the verb "kuzikitizga" to articulate but slowly, or to read aloud but slowly.

'zikitizge' is in reference to the act of articulating slowly. If repeated, *'zikitizge-zikitizge'* is in reference to a steady contibuous act of articulation.

"Ŵakati ŵamupa kalata kuti waŵazge kumadoda, iye mbwenu kalata yila zikitizge pakaŵazga."

"Kuti bamupulike makola, mbwenu Temwanani makani ghala zikitizge/zikitizge-zikitizge pakayowoya."

Zikizge[2]

This is from the verb "kuzikizga" to chase, or to chase away.

'zikizge' is in reference to a single act of chasing. If repeated, *'zikizge-zikizge'* is in reference to a done deal: the chasing or the chasing away has been done.

"Ŵalendo ŵati ŵafika, mbwenu tambala yula zikizge."

"Chifukwa chakukwiya, a sekulu mbwenu ŵana ŵose zikizge-zikizge pakaya.

Ziliku[2]

This comes from the verb "kuzilika" to writhe, or to wriggle – as if in pain, or about to die.

'ziliku' is in refrence to the single act or movement of writhing. If repeated, 'zliku-ziliku' is in reference to several acts of wriggling – as in an epileptic seizure.

"Mwana tikamuchilikita mpaka mwana ziliku/ziliku-ziliku."

Zilili

This is from the verb "kuzililika" to feel numb, or to be without the sense of feeling.

'zilili' (zirrrri) is in reference to lifelessness in one's limb.

"Awonani namunyinu – kawoko kati waka zilili."

Zinazina

"This is from the noun "chiziulika" or "chizita" the inability to do something quickly.

'zinazina' refers to the act of either indecision, or futility.

"Nyengo yakuti tose tanozgeka, Vitumbiko mbwenu zinazina mpaka ise tikadangilako waka.

Zindu

This is from the verb "kuzinduka" to feel nauseatic.

'*zindu*' refers to the spur of nausea.

"Ndati ndamwa mankhwala, mbwenu mtima zindu."

Zingiliru² or Zunguliru²

This is derived from the verb "kuzingilira" or "kuzungulira" to move in a circle, or to go in a round about way.

'*zingiliru*' or '*zunguliru*' is with reference to the act of: (i) moving in a complee circle, (ii) not acting with speed (iii) not being straight forward (iv) moving without direction. If repeated, '*zingiliru-zingiliru*' or '*zunguliru-zunguliru*' are in reference to continued motions around an object or subject but without a sense of purpose or direction.

"Iwe Phyoka umo wambila zingiliru-zingiliru/pa nyumba ya munyako – kasi nchvichi?"

"Kanandi usange ncheŵe yikukhumba kukhala pasi, yikwamba kuti zingiliru/-zunguliru."

"Zamiwe pakuyowoya mbwenu zingililu-zingililu, na fundo na yimoza!"

Zingilizge²

This is from the verb "kuzingilizga" to encircle.

'*zingilizge*' is in reference to the act of encircling. If repeated, '*zingilizge-zingilizge*' is in reference to total encirclement – such that all gaps for possible escape are sealed.

"Ŵamunkhwele ŵati ŵafwasa, tili nawo zingilizge."

"Mukati mwa usiku, mbwenu ŵalwani chikaya chila zingilizge-zingilizge."

Zingiziwe² or Zingwe²

These are from the verb "kuzingiziwa" or "kuzingwa" to have no one to turn to.

'zingiziwe' or *'zingwe'* is in reference to a state of loneliness and apathy. If repeated, *'zingiziwe-zingiziwe'* or *'zingwe-zingwe'* is in reference to a state of dire helplessness.

"Masozi ŵati ŵamupoka katundu yose, mbwenu zingiziwe/zingwe."

"Mahlazi ŵanyina ŵati ŵatayika, mbwenu mwana zingiziw-zingiziwe/zingwe-zingwe."

Zizike[2]

This is from the verb "kuzizika" to puzzle, or to surprise, or to trick.

'zizike' is in reference to a single act of tricking, or surprising. If repeated, *'zizike-zizike,'* is in reference to repeated acts of fooling, or tricking to the point of one being totally flabbergasted.

"Pakuzgola nyozi kuzgoka njoka, mbwenu Songiso ŵanthu ŵose zizika."

"Mumalo mwakuti walongosole makola, mbwenu Mafunase ŵanyake zizike-zizike."

Zizikike[2]

This is from the verb "kuzizikika" to be puzzled or to be surprised, or to be astonished.

'zizikike' is in reference to one's expression of incomprehension. If repeated, *'zizikike-zizikike'* is in referencet to total disbelief, or total lack of understanding a situation.

"Wati wamanya kuti mwanakazi wake wakwenda uheni, mbwenu Lazalo zizikike/zizikike-zizikike."

Zizimu

This comes from the verb "kuzizimuka" to come to, or regain consciousness – as from sleep or from a coma.

'zizimu' is in refrerence to "the waking up" or "the return to life."

Ŵati bamuthila maji Boti, mbwenu zizimu."

Zizipizge[2]

This is from the verb "kuzizipizga" to persevere, or to move on despite difficulties or hurdles.

'zizipizge' is in reference to the effort of persevering, or continuing on despite problems – as in a failed marriage. If repeated, *'zizipizge-zizipizge'* is in reference to a concerted and continuous effort not to give up.

"Ulanda wati wawona kuti nthengwa yamba kusuzga, mbwenu dankha zizipizge."

"Nanga uli mwanalume wake wakamusuzganga, Khataza mbwenu zizipizge-zizipizge."

Zi-zi-zi/zizime

'zi-zi-zi' is in reference to the feel of cold – as in cold weather, or in cold water, or in cold body. *'zizime'* is in reference to getting cool or cold.

"Maji ghachita kuti zi-zi-zi."

"Tati tasunga maji mu msuku, mbwenu maji ghala zizime."

Zolo

This is from the verb "kuzoloka" to be swampy.

'zolo' is in reference to the sinking into soft mass – as soil.

"Vula yati yawa, mbwenu pasi napo zolo."

Zoto

This is derived from the verb "kuzotola" to inflict a deep wound.

'zoto" is in reference to the appearance of the deep cut.

"Chigomezgo wati watola chisulo, mbwenu pa mutu wa Muwuso zoto."

Zowole[2]

This is from the verb "kuzowola" to punch a hole in an object, or to create punctures on some surface.

'zowole' is in reference to a single act of punching. If repeated, *'zowole-zowole'* is in reference to creating several holes allover some surface.

"Mujancha wati wasanga phunu, mbwenu phuno lila zowole."

"Mumalo mwakuti wapwelele, mbwenu Dumisani chipaso chila zowole-zowole."

Zukuma

This comes from the verb "kuzukuma" to be astounded, or shocked, or overwhelmed with amazement.

'zukuma' is in reference to the state of being astounded beyond belief.

"Wati wapulika za yifwa ya mudumbu wake, Gomezgani mbwenu zukuma."

Zuwulu

This is derived from the verb "kuzuwuluka" to lack colour and taste – as in a soup that has no dressing and without taste, or as in a saltless dish.

'zuwulu' is thus in reference to that tastelessness, or that lack of colouring. Euphemistically, *'zuwulu'* can also be applied in reference to the lack of conviction in an argument or discource.

"Dende nalilawa ndipo lachita kutu zuwulu."

"Fundo zako zikuchita kuti zuwulu – ukaŵenge wamunyake, mphanyi waleka waka kuyowoya."

Zwanyu

This is from the verb "kuzwanyula" to bite off a chunk.

'zwanyu' is thus in reference to the act of biting off a big piece.

"Apo Kholiwe wakatenge wapona, ng'ona yili naye zwanyu."

Zwatu

This stems from the verb "kuzwatula" to violently bite off a large chunk of muscle.

'zwatu' is in reference to the act of biting off and leaving a gaping wound.

"Uko mphoyo yikuchimbila, mphumphi yili nayo zwatu mu nthumbo."

Zwe²

This is from the verb "kuzweta" to take a turn, or to take a long route, or to by-pass.

'zwe' is in reference to the act of taking a turn, or the act of by-passing or taking a detour. If repeated, *'zwe-zwe'*, this is in reference to continuously turning turns.

"Mumalo ŵakuti Yesaya wanjile mu nyumba, mbwenu kuseli kwanyumba zwe."

"Apo galu yikatenge yakola kakalulu, mbwenu kakalulu kala zwe."

"Apo tikaghanaghananga kuti tose tinamaghanoghano ghamoza, mbwenu munyithu zwe."

"Mumalo mwakuti musewu wujumphe pakaya, mbwenu musewu wula zwe."

"Umo tayambila zwe-zwe – mwati tamufika po?"

Zwi or Zwitu

These are from the verb "kuzwita" to cram, or to swallow hastily – as with a chunk of food.

'zwi' or 'zwitu' refer to the act of cramming or gulping.

"Kamdidi wati wamenya sima, mbwenu mumulomo zwi/zwitu."

VITHOKOZO

Yebo Mvalo
Wena wa kwa Mkhwamubi
Wena wa kwa Malandula
Wena wa kwa Thimbi-thimbi
Se wa kwa Chiyagaga
Se wa kwa Mhlanga, Semuzilini
Wena wa kwa Magwaza
Ngeziyabamba
Yebo Hwati Hau!!!!

Yebo Madise
Wena wa kwa Lombo
Wena wa kwa Lokothwayo
Wena wa kwa Mazalinkosi
Wena wa kwa Dhlamini
Wena wa kwa Ndwandwa
Wena wa kwa Logenuka
Wena wa kwa Masakasaka

www.ingramcontent.com/pod-product-compliance
Lightning Source LLC
Chambersburg PA
CBHW021711230426
43668CB00008B/794